D1064421

TRIUMPH
BOOKS

MUGGSY

MUGGSY

*My Life from a Kid in the Projects
to the Godfather of Smallball*

Tyrone "Muggsy" Bogues
with Jacob Uitti

TRIUMPH
B O O K S

Copyright © 2022 by Muggsy Bogues and Jacob Uitti

No part of this publication may be reproduced, stored in a retrieval system, or transmitted in any form by any means, electronic, mechanical, photocopying, or otherwise, without the prior written permission of the publisher, Triumph Books LLC, 814 North Franklin Street, Chicago, Illinois 60610.

Library of Congress Cataloging-in-Publication Data

Names: Bogues, Tyrone. | Uitti, Jacob, author.
Title: Muggsy: my life from a kid in the projects to the Godfather of Smallball / Tyrone Bogues, with Jacob Uitti.
Description: Chicago, Illinois: Triumph Books, [2022] | Summary: "A candid and insightful memoir from one the NBA's most unlikely stars. Conversational and clear-sighted, this is a story of uncompromising vision and fleet-footed determination during a golden era for the NBA"—Provided by publisher.
Identifiers: LCCN 2021050850 (print) | LCCN 2021050851 (ebook) | ISBN 9781629379470 (Hardcover) | ISBN 9781637270295 (ePub)
Subjects: LCSH: Bogues, Tyrone | African American basketball players—United States—Biography. | Basketball players—United States—Biography. | African American basketball coaches—United States—Biography. | Washington Bullets (Basketball team)—History. | Charlotte Hornets (Basketball team: 1988–2002)—History. | Toronto Raptors (Basketball team)—History. | National Basketball Association—History. | Stature, Short. | BISAC: SPORTS & RECREATION / Basketball | SPORTS & RECREATION / Coaching / Basketball
Classification: LCC GV884.B64 A3 2022 (print) | LCC GV884.B64 (ebook) | DDC 796.323092 [B]—dc23/eng/20211209
LC record available at https://lccn.loc.gov/2021050850
LC ebook record available at https://lccn.loc.gov/2021050851

This book is available in quantity at special discounts for your group or organization. For further information, contact:

Triumph Books LLC
814 North Franklin Street
Chicago, Illinois 60610
(312) 337–0747
www.triumphbooks.com

Printed in U.S.A.
ISBN: 978-1-62937-947-0
Design by Patricia Frey

———————————————

To my incredible and talented wife, Kim; children, Tyisha,
Brittney, and Ty; brothers, Richard and Anthony; guardian angels
who made everything possible, my mom, Elaine and sister,
Sherron; and first role models, Coach Wade and Leon Howard

—M.B.

To my brilliant and beautiful wife, Eva; twin-brother-
in-law, Cedric; brother, David; mom, Michelle; and
first pick-up pick-and-roll point guard, Jason

—J.U.

———————————————

CONTENTS

FOREWORD

MY DAD PLAYED WITH MUGGSY IN CHARLOTTE, AND MY BROTHER, SETH, and I got to tag along, be in the locker room, and see all of his teammates before and after practice and games. I think there's actually a video of him doing the airplane thing, where he's flying me around the locker room. I was probably around five or six, but I'm not exactly sure.

We grew up with their family: Muggsy's son, Ty, and daughter, Brittney. She and I were in the same kindergarten class at school. (It's now called Charlotte Prep.) Brittney was actually my first crush! Muggs and my dad would come and pick us up from school. It's cool to think how they played on the Hornets together and the whole deal. Every game was amazing. My brother and I didn't get to go to games on school nights. That was the rule. But Fridays and Saturdays were something we looked forward to all week. Part of that was because of the family section in the arena. There was a family room, which was probably as much fun as the actual games. All the kids just hung out. We could come out and watch the game if we wanted to, but sometimes we'd just stay in the back and see everyone later in the tunnel and the locker room.

I remember how electric the city was back then for sure. I loved watching Muggsy play because it was all about the determination and the grit. It's probably been said over and over again, but anybody that can be 5'3" and hang with that level of talent—that's all heart. I gravitated toward that.

When you're a kid, you're like, *All right, 5'3". How much longer until I'm 5'3" and then maybe I can play in the NBA?* I was always keeping tabs on that.

From an eye test, we were just always in amazement because we'd see these broad, giant guys, and then we'd see Muggs running around, stealing the ball, and running as fast as he could down the court, setting guys up. It was just fun to watch, but I also couldn't believe I was watching it.

Our families were very close. Where we were in Charlotte, we'd go over to their house, and they'd come over to ours. We lived in two different neighborhoods, but there was always an obvious connection because our dads had the same schedules and were in the same profession. We all enjoyed the time we got to hang out. Even to this day, my brother and Ty are extremely close. It's pretty cool how long it's lasted.

When we'd go to Hornets practices as a kid, Muggsy would entertain us. We'd play one-on-one. He'd push me around a little bit, but he'd also take it easy and make sure I had fun. But the biggest influence he had was when I was probably 14 or 15. I was just starting to really find my way in high school basketball. I was looking forward to trying to play in college. We were at the gym one day, and he started to lecture me on core strength. He said, "I know you're not going to be the biggest, most athletic, strongest guy." And obviously he wasn't either.

He always talked about making sure your core was the strongest thing in your body so that you could take the hits, so you could handle the physicality. Obviously, hearing that was a big difference-maker and a major reason for how he made it in the league and lasted as long as he did. I took his advice. What he said to me about core strength is something I still think about to this day. It gave me the confidence that I could actually play at the next level. On top of all that, Muggsy has always got such great energy. Whenever you see him, he's smiling and he'll call you, "Young fella." He just makes you feel good.

Muggsy never really took himself too seriously, even though he knew—and we all knew—what kind of impact he had on other people. Anybody who loves basketball and played in the league respects and appreciates his career. Whenever his name pops up, it's usually a fun conversation, talking about somebody who played NBA basketball at 5'3". You have to pay your respect to the guys who accomplished something that remarkable.

These days smallball has taken a new narrative because of how teams are put together with positionless basketball. But I don't think there will ever be another Muggsy. I'm pretty certain there will never be another 5'3" guy that is as successful as he was. He transcends the game because of that. He set the bar. Even now, he's still doing amazing work. He's an ambassador for the league. He'd doing great things in the community here in the U.S. and abroad. He's well-received everywhere. Muggs transcends basketball.

—Stephen Curry, all-time three-point leader and three-time NBA champion

FOREWORD

I FIRST MET MUGGSY BOGUES IN OCTOBER OF '92. I'D JUST FINISHED MY contract negotiation and I'd unfortunately missed training camp and the first four games of my rookie season. The Charlotte Hornets had drafted me, but there were delays in the contract negotiations. I'd been patiently waiting to join the team, but I was also anxious about meeting my new teammates. Finally, though, the deal got done. That morning Hornets officials took me to the team plane. I couldn't even go to my hotel room because our next game was that night on the road in Indiana against the Pacers. When I walked on the plane, I was expecting a warm welcome. But instead everyone just looked at me. They seemed mad as if I was holding thing up.

It was quiet. But the first person who spoke to me was Muggs. I sat down next to him. And from there, he took me under his wing. It was amazing. I was the tallest, biggest guy on the team, and the smallest guy on the team and in the league took me under his wing. He helped me chill out. Muggs got me settled in as a professional. Muggsy gave me direction, which meant a lot for me. It really did, especially on that first day. I'm very thankful and grateful for Muggsy's gesture on the plane. I'm grateful that Muggsy was able to see something in me as a person, too, and for him to take the time to welcome me to the group. He got me acclimated and in the right frame of mind for playing with the Hornets and for playing against the Pacers that night.

There was a tremendous amount of respect for Muggsy at all times. From Day One on the Hornets, Muggsy was sincere. He said that all he wanted was to see me do well and he made that happen. In practices he was the floor general. The one thing he used to tell me was: "Don't let me beat you down the court." Because he was so fast, he would push the basketball up the floor, but he wanted us in front of him to finish on fast breaks. He was an expert at identifying who was open. He got the ball in the right hands at the right time. Muggsy said, "Just don't let me get in front of you. Run as hard as you can. I'll find you. Don't worry about that. I'll find you."

So I did what he told me to do. I sprinted up the court and I was the beneficiary of a lot of his assists. Muggsy made me a better player by just calming me down and helping me understand my strengths, which would in turn help the team win. Once I embraced the direction he was giving me, the rest is history. I was able to build a certain level of confidence because of what he communicated. I could feel that he had confidence in me, which helped me with finding my role and starting my career off the right way. As a rookie and in my second and third year, I had no doubts whatsoever about playing with Muggsy. He was our point guard. I was extremely confident when he was on the floor. He wasn't about anything but making the right play. All you had to do was get yourself open, and he would find you. It was simple as that. Muggsy made it look easy.

Some guys have tough transitions into the league, but mine went a lot smoother than it could have. Despite being the smallest guy on the floor, Muggsy also demanded the most respect because he had the ball in his hands most of the time. He was often the most admired. It was an exciting time for us all together with the Hornets. As we began to win and make the playoffs, I was happy for the city of Charlotte. The city embraced us. We broke a lot of attendance records. During my rookie season, it was almost like we felt that playing well and making the playoffs was our way of showing appreciation for the city's support. It was a very exciting time in a state where basketball has some deep roots.

We were celebrated in Charlotte every time we stepped on the court. So, when we made the playoffs for the first time in franchise history during my rookie season—and with Muggsy being our starting point guard—it was very special. Then we also won the first playoff series, and that really catapulted the popularity of our team. Though I only spent three years in Charlotte with the Hornets, they were tremendously fun years. I treasure that time because those years set the foundation for the rest of my basketball life. The relationships I had with my teammates and the coaches and, most importantly, the city of Charlotte is something that I carry with me. They were truly a difference-maker in my basketball career, and Muggsy was at the heart of it.

Muggsy was like a little big brother. He was always there for me and for the guys on the team. I'm grateful and thankful to call him a friend. Even after I left Charlotte to play in Miami, Muggsy and I kept in touch often. He would come down to play in my charity golf tournaments. And Muggsy is a great golfer.

But to be the smallest guy in the game as a basketball player, it would be easy to be intimated. Muggsy, though, was fearless. He was determined that people weren't going to take advantage of him because of his size. As a player, Muggsy had a lot of fight, and I really respected that. He was a tough guy from Baltimore, and you could feel the competitiveness. It was contagious. It bled into all of us as his teammates.

It was all part of just going out there to war with Muggsy because we felt like if he could do it against all these trees, then we definitely had to step up and do our part. Muggsy's greatest asset as a player was being a tremendous floor general and controlling the game and making the right play each and every time down the court. People don't realize it, but Muggy led the league in assist-to-turnover ratio almost every year. He was one of the smartest players in the NBA. He was confident.

I have so many favorite moments playing with Muggsy. There are so many highlight moments for me in my basketball life thanks to him. But the long and short of it is, there was always a tremendous respect factor around the league for Muggsy. Some may have first looked at him and saw his size, but people were just in awe because of what he was able to do.

—Alonzo Mourning, Naismith Memorial Basketball Hall of Famer

INTRODUCTION

MUGGSY BOGUES IS A MIRACLE. LET'S START THERE. FIRST AND FOREMOST, that's why he should be inducted into the Naismith Memorial Basketball Hall of Fame. Though he was never an All-Star, he's done something no All-Star has done. That's the second reason. In truth, you can't tell the story of the NBA without him. Muggsy is so important to the NBA that he also transcends the very game of basketball. His story is total and complete inspiration—rooted in that round orange rubber ball that he handled so well in the league for 14 seasons. Muggsy is a walking, talking biopic. People say Muggsy can't make the Hall as a player, instead only as a contributor. But what he contributed to the game during his career has been something no one before or after has replicated. His name still rings out.

Muggsy is the shortest player ever to play in the NBA. Muggsy was also born into the inner city of Baltimore where violence and the crack epidemic, which ravaged so many American cities, would quickly do the same to his beloved hometown. But despite being just 5'3", Muggsy rose from that situation to become one of the country's best young point guards. His high school team, the Dunbar Poets, is often understood to be the best high school basketball team in history, and Muggsy was the captain of that ship for each game of the team's back-to-back undefeated seasons.

Later, Muggsy enrolled at Wake Forest University and set a number of university and ACC records by the end of his four-year career. In 1987 the

Washington Bullets drafted Muggsy in the first round (12th overall) in the NBA draft just behind Horace Grant and Reggie Miller and a few spots ahead of New York City point guard legend Mark Jackson. But Muggsy's story took a historic turn when he landed on the 1988 expansion Charlotte Hornets just a year later. There, he would rise to worldwide popularity with the likes of Alonzo Mourning, Larry Johnson, and longtime friend Dell Curry.

Since Muggsy and Dell were so close, their families grew up together. Their kids were close friends. Dell's oldest son, Stephen, was the first person to ever give Brittney Bogues (Muggsy's middle daughter) a diamond ring. Muggsy's son, Ty Jr., was in Seth Curry's wedding and vice versa. The families remain close today. But in Charlotte, where Steph and Seth grew up, Muggsy was one of the Currys' first basketball professors. He showed the young boys how to play bigger than their frames. He showed them how to run a team. Two decades later, Steph would become the supernova core of the NBA's signature smallball movement. But who do you think taught Steph many of its tenets? Muggsy Bogues, aka the Godfather of Smallball.

While helping him write this book, I learned a few things. No. 1: Muggsy was a leader from his heart to his hand. He took giants like Mourning, L.J., Vince Carter, and Tracy McGrady under his wing and helped guide their teams to the playoffs. He led by uniting and inspiring the people around him. Also, Muggsy is a great father and family man. Family is deeply important to him. Though he and his family have been through the proverbial ringer, they've prevailed together. Sadly, when Muggsy was a teenager, his father went to prison for armed robbery. He later died as a result of an addiction to drugs. Muggsy's older brother, Chuckie, is also in recovery.

Muggsy lost his mother in 2001 and retired from basketball that same year. He lost his sister in 2015. Through all the ups and downs, Muggsy's love for his family and, especially, his three kids never waned. When you ask his children—Tyisha, Brittney, and Ty Jr.—they rave about their father, his parenting, the amount of attention he gave them, the life lessons, and the random pop-ins at school (where the staff and students would shriek with glee seeing a famous athlete their height or shorter). For almost his entire life, Muggsy has taken care of his family—from buying his mother a house to offering his to Chuckie as a place to rehabilitate.

Although the first image of a looming Godfather might not be the diminutive Muggsy Bogues, in truth he certainly fits the bill for this story. Muggsy is the shortest basketball player ever to play in the NBA. As a result, he was also a marketer's dream. The Hornets' teal jackets and jerseys were everywhere in the '90s, as ubiquitous as Michael Jordan and Kurt Cobain. When he played later in his career for the expansion Toronto Raptors, Muggsy brought the crowd out there, too. Kids love him. But more than the 14 years he gave the NBA, the magnitude of his impact is felt still today.

There have been tens of thousands of players to play in the NBA, but a small percentage has ever averaged a double-double. Muggsy did it when he averaged 10.8 points and 10.2 assists in 1993–94. Few have retired in the top 20 of any category. When he retired Muggsy left the game with the 13th most career assists. Not many people have ever played 82 games in a season. Muggsy did it in 1991–92 (the same season he was name-dropped by A Tribe Called Quest in a song). Muggsy also averaged two steals or more three times, started on multiple playoff teams, and finished two seasons with a top 15 offensive rating (1994–95 and 1996–97). But more than any numbers, Muggsy's reputation was the gleaming star of his NBA life. He was as respected as any player in the league. His mere existence was triumph.

Muggsy was a big celebrity. He was in *Space Jam* with Jordan. He was also in *Eddie* with Whoopi Goldberg and on episodes of *Saturday Night Live* with Nirvana, *Hang Time* with Anthony Anderson, and *Curb Your Enthusiasm* with Larry David. He coached in the WNBA and inspired countless players in the league, many of whom were around his height. In a way Muggsy was something like basketball's Forrest Gump in that he's touched almost every significant moment in history—from Moses Malone to Michael Jordan to Kobe Bryant, Carter, and LaMelo Ball. Muggsy never won an NBA MVP and he was never even an All-Star (though he should have been). The only statistical category he led was the unglamorous assist-to-turnover ratio. He never won an NBA championship. Yet, plenty have won those things, and we don't remember their names. Everyone knows the name Muggsy Bogues.

As you read this book, you'll see how he did that through stories from his closest friends and family and from Muggsy himself. These will show that he was someone who could do more than what others thought of him. Yet, despite all this, Muggsy almost never made it past five years old. He survived a near-deadly gunshot. He still has the scars to remember it. But Muggsy was undeterred by the incident. Rather, he was bolstered by his survival. That's who he is. In a way Muggsy's story has always been about growth. When you're a 5'3" professional basketball player, you have to earn every inch because you're at such a relative disadvantage. But in truth Muggsy never saw himself at a disadvantage. That's why he succeeded despite the tallest odds.

—*Jacob Uitti*

MUGGSY

THICK SKIN

I CAN STILL REMEMBER MY FIRST BASKETBALL. I GOT IT AS A PRESENT when I was three years old. Of course, some 20 years later, I'd be the starting point guard for the National Basketball Association's Charlotte Hornets. Standing there at 5'3", the shortest player ever to do it in a game full of giants, on the hardwood with some of the best of all time, I'd guard the likes of Michael Jordan, Kevin Johnson, Gary Payton, and John Stockton. But even more than the day I was drafted on June 22, 1987 or the game when I blocked the shot of the 7'0" center and New York Knicks great Patrick Ewing, I can remember getting my very first basketball. I can still see it in my hands right now clear as day. It was bigger than I was.

That red-and-white Wilson all-purpose rubber ball was a gift from my Godmother on Christmas. I was born just three years earlier on January 9, 1965. Even by three, I knew to expect small gifts around the turn of each year in winter. But that first basketball was something special. I immediately pumped it with air and took it down to the chilly outdoor asphalt courts. I loved it as soon as I put my hands on the rubber seams. But that didn't mean I could control it. Not at first anyway. The new ball was so bouncy that I couldn't get a handle on it. I'd lose control of it in the house or down the hallway or dribbling it while taking out the trash. I'd fumble it as I ran from the steps of the Baltimore housing projects, where we lived, to the nearby outdoor basketball courts, where the neighborhood kids played pick-up games. For me, the ball was like a yo-yo except I had yet to build the string.

For the first three years of my life, my family and I lived on the 10th floor of the redbrick 1035 building in the Lafayette Court high-rise housing projects. It was on Orleans Street in East Baltimore not far from the city's downtown. But when I was three years old and right around the time that I got that first basketball, we moved from the high-rise apartments to the next-door low-rise building, which was across the street from the neighborhood rec center. Once I started playing at the rec center around eight or nine years old, that was my home away from home. The rec center changed my life.

Our family's apartment in the low-rise building was small but cozy. Thinking about it today, I can remember darn near every inch and all five rooms. When you walked in, the kitchen was on the left, and the living room—where my parents, Elaine and Richard Bogues, put up my trophies and the photos of us kids—was to the right. My parents' room was adjacent to the kitchen, and my brothers and I all shared a room next to them. My sister, Sherron, had her own room next to us. My parents raised us well. They instilled in us the love of family. In our family we're all short, and everyone has nicknames. That's us. My grandfather, who stood well short of 6', was Richard, but everyone called him "Snook." My dad, who was 5'5", was also Richard, but everyone called him "Bill." His eyes and smile could light up a room. My mom, who was 4'11", never wanted to be called "Mom," so we called her "Lainey" most of the time. Her face just radiated warmth. Over the years, my parents were present for our lives, which was a blessing. My mom was the backbone of our family. She was supportive and encouraging. She'd given birth to me even after two failed pregnancies. She was always my shoulder to cry on when the neighborhood kids bullied me for being short or when they chose not to pick me for games on the playground. I'd hear, "What do you think you're doing, Tyrone? You're too short to play!" Then they'd bust out laughing.

But my mom would tell me to go back out. "No one knows how big your heart is," she'd say. "No one knows what you're capable of. If you want to play, go ahead and play."

The more I heard it, the more I believed it. My mom didn't know much about basketball, but she knew what it took to survive in the world. Thankfully, too, I can still remember her cooking. She'd fry pork chops in a pan in our little yellow kitchen. She'd always keep bologna and hot dogs in the refrigerator and an assortment of cereal in the pantry like Cheerios and Fruity Pebbles. Her specialty was her crab legs, though she'd only let me have the claws when I was little. For dessert she cooked sweet potato pie or her world-famous rice pudding. To this day, I don't eat anyone else's rice pudding except hers. But in our apartment, I also remember keeping our cereal boxes closed tight so the cockroaches wouldn't get in while we slept. I used to hate to turn the light on in the morning and see those things scurry.

The area of Baltimore, where I grew up, has experienced a lot of change over the decades. But in the early years of my life, the place always felt like home. Neighbors were friendly; we knew each other's names and families. Later, however, as regional industries began to lay off workers just as the crack cocaine epidemic swept through major cities, including and especially Baltimore, the area became rougher and more dangerous. There had always been difficulty and danger around to navigate. But after crack came in, things felt more desperate. I once saw someone get shot on the basketball court right in front of me. Shot in the head. We were playing, and this guy was just going for a lay-up when—*BOOM*— he dropped. We ran. A few years later, I saw a man get beaten to death with a baseball bat. It was horrible. I never wanted to see anything like that ever again. I wish I could get these memories out of my brain now, to be honest.

When I was five years old, I was shot, too. I was staying up past my bedtime one night when I heard some commotion outside on the street. For some reason, I went downstairs and outside to check it out. At one point, a man threw a brick through the window of Old Man Chester's soul food restaurant. The brick shattered the window. It was like everything happened in slow motion. Old Man Chester ran out of his place with a shotgun, angry as all hell. He began firing. Someone shouted, "It was those kids!" And Chester took aim at me and my sister, Sherron, who was also in the crowd now with me. We ran. There was no room for reasoning with Chester. He pulled the trigger, and the buckshot hit me in the arm, leg, and side. I still have some of it left in my arm today to remember 50 years later. But despite my size and age, I survived, though I'd lost a lot of blood. When I opened my eyes later in the hospital, I thought for a moment I was dead, staring into the light. When you grow up in the inner city, you tend to expect that sort of thing.

Questions raced through my brain in the hospital room. In a way, I was surprised I woke up at all. I was fortunate enough that it was only the buckshot—not a complete bullet—that got me. If I'd been bigger, it might have gotten a more vulnerable internal organ. I wondered *Why me? Am I going to make it?* The doctors said that they couldn't remove all of the buckshot because it was all in so deep. But they said it would fall out over time on its own, and it mostly has. In the hospital when I regained consciousness with the doctors and nurses all around me, I was told that I'd pull through okay. But the memory has stayed with me ever since—that moment of deep fear. Coming back from the buckshot, however, also gave me a new sense of courage I'd never felt before. Just like a radioactive spider had bit Spider-Man, Baltimore buckshot got me. And I was stronger for it.

I'd already heard the stuff from the other kids for years—even by five years old. But now those insults bounced off me. I'd survived a bullet. I could survive them, too. Of course, my parents were furious at Chester. I thought my dad might try to kill the guy that day (Chester was lucky the cops got him before my dad did). But thanks to my mom, cooler heads prevailed. I tried to forget all about it. I brushed it off.

In the apartment my brothers and I would watch TV to pass the time on rainy days. We'd sit on the couch, which was covered with crinkly protective plastic along with a lot of our furniture in the apartment. Often I was the one who had to hold the coat hanger we used as a TV antenna to get reception. When we weren't watching TV, we played games, betting our spare change or candy. I was very close with my siblings. Boy, we were loud in that house.

For peace, mom had to get us to play outside. With each day I fell more and more in love with basketball. In fact, I got my first pair of basketball shoes at five years old, and there was no stopping me from there. For basketball players, shoes are the most important element and even more important than the basketball itself. Usually, in a pinch, someone has a ball lying around to use. But shoes are such personal objects. My first were all white Chuck Taylors, the floppy canvas high-tops. By five I'd worn sneakers, of course. But this was my first pair of *basketball* shoes. There's something magical about that. They may not actually be able to make you jump higher or run faster, but they sure feel like they can. I remember being a little kid coming down to the court with my basketball and new shoes on. I had no real control of the ball. I just wanted to get down there and be like everybody else.

But when no one picked me to play in the games, I had to work on my skills in different ways. When the community doesn't accept you, you hope family will be there. Thankfully, our family was tight-knit. Even today when I think about my mom, dad, brothers, and sister, I get choked up. When my mom passed in 2001 from cancer, I retired from the NBA with three years still left on my contract. When my sister died in 2015, I was devastated. Sherron, who we called "Helen," was a heck of a player, too. She and I used to go at it one-on-one all the time as kids inside and outside of the house. I would bend another coat hanger into a hoop and tape it to the doorframe. We'd shoot balled-up socks and try to dunk on each other until lights out at 9:00 PM. The two of us would battle outside, too. We would tie milk crates to the chain-link fence and shoot.

That's how I first started to practice my jump shot in the harsh Baltimore weather. Sherron was a similar player to me. She was a small guard. She was pesky out there, doing her thing. She would often beat me when we played when we were little. After all, she was older than I was. She used to get me before I got good. But then when I got to her level, she couldn't beat me anymore. I laugh, remembering us going at it one-on-one. She was the first person to help me really sharpen my game. Sherron later played at Dunbar (where I would later star). She was so good that she later played at Towson State in college. When I played at Dunbar, she was my biggest cheerleader. She would yell from the stands for me to shoot or to listen to what my coaches were telling me.

In her professional life after her playing days, Sherron had an award-winning 32-year career with the Baltimore City Parks Department, helping people from everyday folks to future NBA pros like University of Maryland star Juan Dixon. Sherron helped me believe that even when the other kids were negative that I was good enough to be in the game. She told me to go out there and prove them all wrong. Many years later, after Sherron passed, then-Baltimore mayor Stephanie Rawlings-Blake decreed that June 27th was Sherron Bogues Day in Baltimore. That was a testament to Sherron's impact. Ever since her passing, I've held annual summer basketball and football tournaments on June 27 in Baltimore in her honor. Though I was the youngest and smallest in the family, Sherron always said I could do whatever I wanted to.

I wouldn't be who I am today without Sherron. Growing up, my brothers and I liked to roughhouse in our room. We slept in our crowded, burgundy-painted bedroom and were always talking about something or another. My oldest brother Richard, who everyone called "Chuckie," had his own bed while my other older brother Anthony, who everyone called "Stroh," and I shared a bunk bed. (I was on the top bunk.) Stroh was four years older than I, and Chuckie was three years older than Stroh. It was tight quarters in those years, but the three of us made the best of it. We had our fair share of spats, and there were plenty of times when our dad had to come in and tell us to quiet the heck down, but in the end, it brought us closer together.

We all played sports. It was something to fill the days, but we also loved it. Chuckie was the only one who didn't really take to basketball. Stroh was a standout basketball player. He was also a great running back for the Dunbar football team. Sometimes when the other kids picked on me, Chuckie and Stroh would make sure to step in to defend me. They were great older brothers. To support them, I'd go watch their games at Dunbar. As a result, I got to know the programs before I even attended and the coaches, too. I loved playing sports. I excelled at baseball, wrestling, football, Ping-Pong, and basketball. When I was eight years old, I got so good at Ping-Pong that I won a city rec league championship. As I'd started to play the game, I could barely see over the table. A few years later, I was the champion.

Even though we loved sports, my parents made sure we went to school and attended our classes. After school we'd come home, and they made sure we did our homework first before we could go out. When we were through, we'd hit the rec center to play. Around 12 years old, I stopped growing. Truthfully, I don't remember not being 5'3". It feels like I've always this height. I joke that my mom was the first woman to give birth to a 5'3" baby. But when I was young, it was hard. My mother was my hero. She told me not to listen to the other kids. "God doesn't make mistakes," she said.

Most of all, what I wanted to do was show people what I was capable of on the court. Yet I had people throughout my life tell me what I should do instead. First, it was wrestling. I'd won a lot of tournaments already and I'd shown an aptitude for it. Then it was baseball or football. Anything but basketball. But I loved basketball most. I was driven to succeed at it.

That didn't mean the insults stopped. Sticks, stones, and buckshot can hurt. Words can, too. Thankfully, my mom was there for me. She would tell me that no one could control my life but me. She would say just because I was smaller didn't mean I was worse than anyone else. My father was supportive, too. But as I got older, he was around less. He'd stopped staying at the house as often as he used to. My neighborhood may have felt like home, but it also had its fair share of difficulties to navigate. Today East Baltimore has seen revitalization in some parts while others have continued to fall by the wayside. The project homes, where I grew up, have been turned to rubble. In the 1970s it wasn't easy to get by for people in the inner city. The life expectancy of someone like me or my father was about 20 years old. My father knew how tough the streets were. For much of my young life, he focused on trying to earn a living. He was always present on holidays, but as I got older, he became more involved in the streets.

Sadly, when I was 12 years old, he was sent away to prison to the Jessup Correctional Institution for armed robbery. Baltimore is famous for its ports and the ships that bring cargo to them. My dad was one of the men who offloaded those ships. He had been what they called a stevedore or longshoreman. My father worked the docks with a lot of other guys, lugging cargo to trucks that would take the stuff away to stores and warehouses in the area. He was a good worker. But as the years passed, work became more and more scarce, and as Baltimore and our neighborhood, in particular, began to deteriorate, my father wasn't able to avoid the temptation to make a quick dollar. He started getting high regularly, too, sometimes with my brother, Chuckie. He hustled odd jobs, some of which were illegal. He was trying to take care of his family and in some ways he was doing an okay job. But the lifestyle caught up with him. He was sentenced to 20 years behind bars. Devastated, we had to pick up the pieces.

My mom visited him every weekend. She was his saint. I couldn't bring myself to do it. I regret that now. But it was how I had to cope. I was angry. I resented him for leaving. He'd let us down. To pick up the slack, my mother had to go on public assistance. She'd dropped out of high school in 11ᵗʰ grade, but in order to put food on the table and keep the lights on, she decided to go back and get her G.E.D. After that, she started working in a healthcare facility as an administrative assistant to support us in my dad's absence. Though she was a single mother, she made sure to take care of us. We always had good clothes and shoes. As she worked herself to the bone, I focused on basketball. Though I was much shorter than most of the other kids, I began to exhibit special talents on the court. I was showing a great deal of promise as a point guard, and people were beginning to notice. My height began to matter less and less. I thrived on the court.

As I got into my teens, I learned just how fast I could race ahead of every other player, pushing the pace of the game like no one else in the city. I told myself: *keep your head up*. I was a blur between the lines. No one else saw the game from my perspective, and I used that to my advantage every chance I could. On the playgrounds growing up, the neighborhood kids began to accept me. Once they finally saw what I could do in a game, I became one of the top picks amongst them. I honed my skills, learning to look for the big guys as they ran the lanes. I loved to push the ball ahead of everyone on a fast break. I wanted to find my teammates, get them the ball at the perfect moment, and watch as they scored on the other team. That might be my favorite thing in the whole world.

But finally getting accepted into the games wasn't enough. I wanted to be the best of all the kids my age. It had taken me so long to get into the games that what I wanted to stand out like the greats in the neighborhood, people like Larry Gibson, Skip "Honeydip" Wise, and Dwayne Wood.

They were stars at Dunbar High School. Honeydip's team beat DeMatha High School and the future two-time NBA scoring champ, Adrian Dantley. Wood, who would later play college ball at Virginia State, was a few years older than I. But I watched everything he could do. He was a smaller guard like me. He was about 5'6". But by watching him, I was able to hone my game. There wasn't anyone small like me playing basketball on TV. The guy they called "Tiny" Archibald on the Boston Celtics was 6'1", so I looked to Wood for clues. Later, I'd play at Dunbar with his nephew, Darryl, and we'd tear it up together.

Wood could do everything, but I loved how he could run a team. He made guys better, and that's a part of the game that's too often overlooked. Just like I used to go at it one-on-one with Sherron with the balled-up socks, I went at it with Wood on the court day in and day out. He was the person I measured myself against. Sometimes we'd play one-on-one *full court* to build our stamina. Those were tough ones. Wood was lightening quick and very skilled. I did my best to emulate him, learning as we played each day. Wood could do anything a big guard could. He could shoot pass, dribble, get by a defender, and orchestrate a team. He was fast and could defend with the best. Wood was a natural in the fast break. He could slice through the lane or hit a foul-line jump shot. He was small, but he was successful. That's what I wanted to be, too.

Wood was a star at Dunbar and played in college. But in my humble opinion, he never followed through with where his talent could have taken him. He never played in the pros, though he could have. Another guy like that in the neighborhood was Wise. He also was older than I. Wise was maybe the best player ever to come up and play for Dunbar, and that's saying a lot. He would tell younger players like me what to do and not to do in order to have a successful career. He gave us advice. I looked up to Wise. Later, Wise made it to Clemson University and was a star for the program. But he dropped out early to play professional for a little while. Unfortunately, he let drugs derail his life. When I went on to play in the NBA, I thought about how in my own way I was carrying on the legacies of Wise and Wood. Those guys will always be heroes.

While it's true that no one has ever played in the NBA at my height, that doesn't mean little guys have never excelled at the professional game. In the 1940s a few guys played in the league who were pretty short. Mel Hirsch, Wataru Misaka, and Red Klotz were each 5'7". Misaka, who is Japanese, is actually the first non-White player ever to play in the NBA. Later, others around that size would find their way into the league. In 1985, two years before I was drafted, the Atlanta Hawks acquired the 5'7" Spud Webb to play guard after the Detroit Pistons had selected him in the fourth round. Webb, who is still a close friend of mine, won the Slam Dunk Contest the following year. (I'm still jealous of him for that!) But I'm also so grateful for him. I tell Spud all the time that if he didn't play well I may never have been drafted into the league. There are others like Calvin Murphy and Greg Grant. They proved to be valuable players in the NBA at just 5'9" and 5'7", respectively.

In 1999 the 5'5" point guard Earl Boykins made his debut in the league. He had a solid career, playing in 652 games, averaging 8.9 points and 3.2 assists. I loved to see that. From 2002 to 2007, Boykins averaged 11.7 points and 3.9 assists in 24.9 minutes per game. Personally, though I'm proud that I hold the record for shortest player in the NBA, I'd love to see more guys in the league like me or even shorter. Today, there is a group of professional basketball players who all know what it's like to be told, "You're too short to play!" But before me that didn't really exist. I'm happy to say I helped the guys who came around after me. I'm proud that I got to help mentor them so that they didn't have to go through what I did. That includes players like two-time All-Star Isaiah Thomas and Slam Dunk Contest champion Nate Robinson.

It helps to share stories with people who've had similar experiences and it makes me happy to see their successes. Even players who were a little bit taller like Allen Iverson, Trae Young, and Steph Curry have helped to show that guys can still dominate in the league even if they aren't 7'0" tall giants. To see someone come into the league today at 5'2" would set my world on fire. The NBA is always going to be defined by its tallest skilled players from George Mikan to Bill Russell, Kareem Abdul-Jabbar, Shaquille O'Neal,

Hakeem Olajuwon, David Robinson, Alonzo Mourning, Tim Duncan, Kevin Durant, and Joel Embiid. But that doesn't mean some of us nongiants can't hoop it up with the best of them. If you can play, you can play. That's always been the best thing about sports. It's a meritocracy.

The problem is people don't always see past their own preconceptions, their own shortcomings. It shouldn't matter the height of a player if he or she can get their teammates the ball, hit the open shot, and stop their opponent from scoring. That's why the only thing that's ever stood in my way was the absence of an opportunity. Once I got in the game, I knew I could play. If I could do it then, knowing that the deck was stacked against me, then that means others can, too. That's why I'm thankful for my childhood in Baltimore. I know it wouldn't be where most people would choose to grow up, but it provided me the experiences I needed to become the person I would become later in life. It may seem odd to say that about a place with so many boarded up houses today, but Baltimore was home and I'm proud of it.

MEMORY LANE
Anthony "Stroh" Bogues

"When we lived in the projects, we used to go up to the top floor of the high-rise building. We would play little games up there on the 11th floor. There were these three little square windows up there, too, and you could stand on the middle one. Up on the ceiling was this pole. You could jump from the window to try to grab the pole and swing and hang from it. So, Muggsy did that one day. But when he jumped, he missed the pole and fell straight down. I thought he was dead! I said to myself, 'Oh my god, my mother is going to kill me!' But Muggs was fine!"

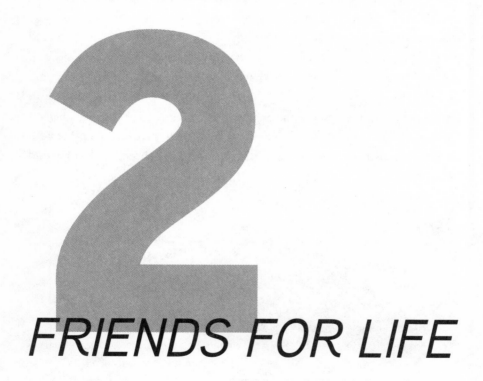

2

FRIENDS FOR LIFE

IN HIS PRIME REGGIE WILLIAMS, WHO I ALWAYS CALLED "RUSS," STOOD 6'7" tall. Russ was a full foot-and-a-half taller than I, but we've been best friends ever since the day we met as kids. We've always treated each other as equals on and off the court. I remember meeting Russ at the rec center, but he says he remembers meeting when we tried out for the wrestling team. Either way, we bonded quickly and became as close as brothers. Our older siblings knew each other already. So even if we weren't playing hoops, we were always around one another. Throughout our lives our friendship has helped us immensely—from our early days as kids, through the pros, and now into our retirement. But when we met, we were so young that we could barely make a jump shot on a 10-foot rim. Yet, we practiced every day.

At the time in the city of Baltimore, each housing project was required to have a recreation center built adjacent to it for the residents. Unfortunately, that is no longer the case today in the city. But back then the rec center was the most important thing in the world besides my family. It was my oxygen, soil, and sunlight. It was where we played thousands of basketball games through the years. It was there where Russ and I became close and where we'd quickly meet the first important coaches in our lives. In many ways our first coaches there helped to save our lives. They taught us discipline, dedication, and sacrifice, and by extension, that kept us out of trouble. If it wasn't for some of my early basketball coaches, I don't know if I'd be writing this book today.

Growing up, Russ and I went to all the Dunbar High School games. We knew all the team fight songs and we sang them along with the cheer-leaders when we were young. We cheered our older siblings and fell for the great Dunbar program hook, line, and sinker. As friends and as basketball players, Russ and I were supremely compatible. Back then, there was a popular comic strip in the newspapers called *Mutt and Jeff*, and my mom called Russ and me "Mutt and Jeff" all the time because we were inseparable. The first coach to really notice our combined potential was a man named Larry Holley. I was just eight years old, and he was also the first to see past my height and treat me like a person—not a *short* person. I was just a kid when I began to play for Holley, but I'll always remember him giving me the confidence that I needed to take the next step forward.

When you're starting out, you need people to believe in you. Holley was the first coach to do that for me. My next coach was Edgar Bell, who people called "Mr. Lee" and who I called "Tweety Bird." He was a tough but fair guy and an even nicer man. Looking back, one game still makes me cringe. It was a close one, and we were down a few points in the fourth quarter. Tweety Bird took me out in the fourth, and I was so mad that he did that. I've always hated coming out of games. But after the game, Tweety Bird drove me home, and I didn't speak to him. I was still mad when he dropped me off. So, as he pulled away, I threw a rock at his car, and it smashed his windshield. His car stopped, and I was afraid he was going to come out and beat my butt or—worse—tell my parents. But instead he just kept driving. I felt horrible for that, and I made sure I'd never do anything so stupid ever again. He never punished me for it, but he didn't need to. I just felt so freaking low. I just felt so bad once it happened. But no he never punished me. He just swept it under the rug and went to practice next day. I was still the guy, still starting. I wasn't throwing that rock to break his window. It was just out of frustration. Tweety had always provided us with cookies out of his trunk after games. So, I did that right after I'd gotten a few cookies. And I still busted his window. Man, I told him I was so sorry later.

Even when the NBA was just a dream, Russ and I played like it would be a reality. Although Holley and Tweety were the first two coaches to see our potential, it was really Mr. Leon Howard who started to shape us. Russ and I had passion for the game. There was no doubt about that. But as kids, we needed direction to stay focused. Thankfully, we got that from Mr. Howard.

He was the director of the rec center. He ran the place and had the keys to the doors. Every morning before playing, Mr. Howard made us say the Pledge of Allegiance, and I always wanted to be the one to hold the flag in the front of the gym. In us Mr. Howard saw the desire to play and be great. He saw our need to learn. He would even open the gym early just for us so he could make sure we were working hard on the fundamentals. Sometimes he would hold up a broomstick and make me shoot over it. He'd done the same for other talented players before us, but that extra attention made all the difference for Russ and me.

Once Mr. Howard took Russ and me under his wing, everything started to click. In college earlier in his life, Mr. Howard had been a teammate of the great Harlem Globetrotters ballhandler Curly Neal. He knew the kind of discipline it took for anyone to make it out of his hometown and be consistently great. So Mr. Howard made us do all sorts of dribbling, shooting, and passing drills and a lot of conditioning and defensive exercises. We learned to count on him. Russ and I would rely on those basics for the rest of our careers all the way up to the highest level. My legs burned after each practice, but by the time I was 13 years old, we'd already won a city rec league championship, and I was named the MVP of the tournament. I was learning to see the game in a complete way, and it felt good to be recognized for it. Russ and I couldn't be stopped—or so we thought.

Across town on the west side of Baltimore, there was another duo our same age in David Wingate and Reggie Lewis (or "Gate and Truck," as I'd later call them), who played for the famed Cecil Kirk Rec Center. Those two would challenge us for best in the city before we'd all later join up and make Baltimore history. But for the time being, it was just Russ and me. Ever since we were seven years old, we'd been talking about what we'd do on the courts together. We dreamed of winning a city high school championship at Dunbar. We knew we could rise up in Baltimore together. Russ would run the break, and I would get him the ball, often after stealing it from my opponent. I'd pick their pocket, turn on the jets, and dish it up to him. I was especially good on defense. I'd work to sneak up behind anyone dribbling and poke the ball out of his hands.

People found it hard to simply dribble around me. In the open court, I played something of a free safety, roaming the passing lanes for a steal. In fact, I got so good at taking the ball that one day on the playground, Dwayne Wood started saying that I was "mugging" everyone out there on the court. As a result, he started calling me "Muggsy" and so did everyone else in the neighborhood pretty quickly. At first, I didn't like the nickname, I didn't want to be known for "mugging" anyone. That sounded negative. But I learned to love it. As it happened, one of my favorite TV shows at the time was *The Bowery Boys*. The show was about this group of tough guys from New York City from the 1940s, and I watched it every Saturday. The main character in the group was a small guy also named Muggsy. He kept everyone in line. I liked that quality. I was the leader of my guys, too.

So, the nickname stuck. Growing up, my mom called me "Apple" because I kept my hair short so that my head looked like a shiny apple. My whole family called me Apple actually. I was the fourth child and the youngest by far, so everyone thought the nickname was all cute. But it wasn't long before "Muggsy" became my name. Everyone from my family to my teammates to everyone in the neighborhood called me Muggsy. It got to the point where no one knew my name was Tyrone anymore. Later, most of my teammates in the pros never knew my real first name. But having a nickname means you're *somebody* in the community. It meant people noticed you, talked about you. Today, neither my three kids nor my wife Kim calls me Tyrone. They all just call me Muggsy and so do all my friends. On the court, I was Muggsy, the tough-minded, scrappy leader. Tough times don't last, but tough people do.

Back then, we all had nicknames. In a way, it was a rite of passage. Williams was, of course, called Russ and he was so quiet you'd sometimes forget if he was in the room. But if you were to take a glance at his basketball résumé, you'd be amazed at what the quiet guy could do on the court. Russ and I both graduated from high school in 1983, but he did so as the nation's Mr. Basketball, the honor bestowed on the country's best high school player. After graduation Russ went to Georgetown University and played there all four years. He won the 1983–84 national championship, playing a key role in the final game. He was named a consensus first-team All-American when he graduated in 1987. Russ was drafted into the NBA with the fourth overall pick by the Los Angeles Clippers and played in the league for 10 years, averaging 12.5 points, 4.0 rebounds, and 2.5 assists per game. In 1991–92, which was his best season with the Denver Nuggets, Russ averaged 18.2 points, 5.0 rebounds, and 2.9 assists in 81 games. It was an All-Star caliber year. I was so proud of him. He'd worked his behind off for it.

When we were kids, if Russ and I weren't playing basketball, we were hanging at each other's house. He and I are very different people, but I think that's what helped us become such good friends. I never stopped talking back then. I always had a smile on my face, chatting and joking with everyone around me. Talk, talk, talk. But Russ was much more reserved. He wasn't nearly as gregarious as I. Few ever are, to be honest. But Mr. Howard saw something in us that could bloom, a partnership. When he was younger, Mr. Howard was a good player. He was a small guard, so he had sympathy for guys like me. As a young man, Mr. Howard had played at Johnson C. Smith University in Charlotte and did well before coming back to Baltimore to work for the city. He pushed the kids in the neighborhood. There aren't a lot of guys out there who will do that, but Mr. Howard did. He taught us the importance of a team. Those, who took to it, excelled.

As a kid Russ played like a guard. He could dribble and pass almost as well as I could. But later in high school, he got a big growth spurt. While he'd picked up skills from a guard's perspective earlier in his development, learning everything from a smaller person's point of view, almost overnight he shot up to 6'6" and was still growing. He became a big guy able to play above the rim. All of a sudden, he was a powerful forward, looking over top of people and jumping over them, too. But that didn't stop him from working hard and getting better. Although not everyone likes to be pushed, Russ and I did. Our games improved because of it. Mr. Howard kept on us through high school. He had a background in education. He understood what it meant to teach and the satisfaction that can come from seeing someone like Russ and me get to new heights. It wasn't always easy to find strong mentors in Baltimore. It could be hard to find helping hands in a place where poverty and drugs often ran rampant.

Russ and I shot jumpers from sunup to sundown. Some nights I'd be out there shooting until dawn, and sometimes neighbors would shout down at me from their windows to go to sleep, but nobody ever really messed with us. Growing up, I carried a basketball with me wherever I went. It was my security blanket and my bridge to a life outside of Baltimore. As time went on, Russ and I got to know Gate and Truck better, too. They were great Baltimore players. Although I'd met them both around six or seven years old, we became friends years later. Back then, there was no AAU basketball. Instead the best games pitted neighborhood versus neighborhood, rec center versus rec center. Lafayette played Cecil Kirk often, and Russ and I would compete against Gate and Truck all the time. Fortunately for us, we'd always win. But we all got to know each other really well as a result.

Gate and Truck were very talented players. They could score and defend as well as anyone the city had ever seen. They were tall, lanky, smooth, and dominant. They stood out above just about every other player in the city at that time. Gate was a wiry, strong athlete who would later go on to star at Georgetown and play well in the NBA over a 15-year career. Truck was a supernova star in the making. He would go on to become a 20-point scorer and the captain of the prestigious Boston Celtics and, potentially, Michael Jordan's biggest rival before Truck tragically passed away in a gym from a heart condition. But before all that professional history could transpire, we played together on the greatest high school basketball team of all time. We were literally unstoppable.

By the time we were 13 or 14 and headed for high school, we'd all made names for ourselves in the city. I was a solid player by nine or 10, but by the time I got to be a teenager, I was better than nearly everyone around me. I liked being the guy who kept everyone in line. As Russ and I got to know Gate and Truck, we decided that, even though we were from different parts of Baltimore, we should all come together in high school to win championships. The four of us along with the other talented guys—like Gary Graham, who would later captain the University of Nevada-Las Vegas' 1986 Final Four team, and Tim Dawson, who would win Atlantic 10 Rookie of the Year at George Washington University—joked and dreamed about traveling the country, beating other teams. I'd run the break and find these three future pros as they filled the lanes. But before that could happen, I experienced a shock.

At that time, the city school districts had decided to send students to zone schools instead of the schools in their neighborhood. Though Dunbar was a stone's throw from my home, I had to bus miles away to Southern High School, my zone school. I still don't understand why. Maybe the wrestling coach at Southern thought I'd play for him. I tried to appeal, but somehow the school system couldn't locate my transcripts in time. Though Dunbar was a block from the Lafayette projects and though I'd attended Lombard Middle School, which was a feeder school for Dunbar, I was forced to bus miles away to a different location for my first year. I was furious. I had to watch my basketball best friends move on and play at Dunbar while I was forced to bus across the city and go to a different school for the first year of high school. The guidance department at Dunbar had been waiting for my transcripts, but somehow they never showed up. No one knows what happened. Russ' transcripts landed just fine.

My mother and sister had gone down to Southern every other day to see about my transferring to Dunbar, but the school said there was nothing it could do. It made no sense and still bothers me today. I didn't want to play for the team. I wanted to sit out the season at Southern, but right before the games started, I decided to give it a go. However, when I went to try out, the coach of Southern's varsity team wouldn't let me have the chance. Again, it made no sense. It felt like I was living in a bad dream. Every kid on the team said the coach should let me try out, but he said that he had all the players he wanted. Instead, he sent me to the junior varsity. I went to one JV practice and decided it clearly wasn't for me. It was obvious from the first practice that I was no JV player. So, I decided to play winter rec league basketball with Mr. Howard that season and prepare for Dunbar next year.

Southern started off 0–3 and then 0–6, and the team convinced the coach to finally give me a tryout. I still wasn't going to play for them, but Mr. Howard said I should do it for the experience. He said I should see what the speed of the high school game was like before I transferred to Dunbar.

So, I begrudgingly accepted. Of course, I made the team, but even then the Southern coach sat me during my first game with the team. The only thing I could think of was that he must have felt threatened by me. The coach's name was Meredith Smith, and I hated playing for him. I didn't get off the bench until the third quarter of that first game when we were down by 15 points. But thanks to some timely steals, we came storming back. In that game we lost by a bucket, but my performance had made it clear that I was the rightful starter at Southern. I was extraordinarily quick and, when people took me for granted, I made them pay for it instantly.

When people asked me how I could be so good at the game while being so short, I told them that it's simple. Some players play the game above the rim, but not most of them, and even the high-flyers have to dribble the ball. I played low to the ground, so I was at more of an advantage than anyone. The ball is on the floor more than it is in the air. Anyone who wasn't used to playing against me always let their guard down. They would forget about me at some point, and I would creep up from behind and knock the ball away or swat it out of their hands. By the time they knew what happened, I'd be off to the other end of the court with an assist to a teammate.

This was true in the NBA, it was true in rec league, and it was very true at Southern High School. I only played a handful of games that year, but when the season finished, the coach said he expected me back on the team. There was no chance of that. Though shorter than each player on the team, I stood head and shoulders above all in talent. If it wasn't for Coach Meredith, I may have played the whole season for Southern and had some fun. Coach wanted to prove something. But all he proved was how to lose a player like me. I kept my eyes on Dunbar all year. It was a historic school athletically and academically. Dunbar was named after the famous poet and writer, Paul Laurence Dunbar. The son of slaves, Dunbar, who was born in Kentucky in 1872, published his first poems at 16 years old. Later, he penned the immortal line, "I know why the caged bird sings." At the time at Southern, I felt like I knew what he was talking about.

I wasn't where I belonged either or where I wanted to be. Yet, I kept playing the game I loved for a coach I loathed as I watched Russ, Truck, and Gate succeed across the city. They were doing well, but their Dunbar team was missing something crucial: me. The team needed a lead guard. In fact, there was one heartbreak game against Calvert High School that people still talk about. It was a matchup of the best public school versus the best private Catholic school at that time, and Dunbar ended up losing that one in triple overtime. To this day, Dunbar coaches say if I'd been on the team, we would have won easily. I kept hoping to get to Dunbar. I had faith it would happen. But I couldn't leave Southern until after my freshman year finished and I could officially transfer. To transfer to a different Baltimore high school at that time, the school you wanted to go to had to offer a subject that wasn't offered where you were already enrolled. For me that was dentistry.

Everyone always said I had a great smile so, why not learn all about it, right? When I'd finally finished my first (and only) year at Southern, I was ready to leave. Close to the transfer deadline, however, someone told me there was another error. All of a sudden, school officials couldn't find my transcripts for my request to transfer to Dunbar. I almost blew my lid. I thought someone was really trying to sabotage me. Was it Coach Meredith trying to get me to stay and play for his team another year, even though we hated each together? What was going on? Thankfully, at the last minute, my transfer request cleared, and I was able to switch schools. Finally, with everything set, I was going to be a Dunbar Poet. The history of Baltimore basketball would never be the same.

MEMORY LANE
Reggie Williams

"Muggsy was the youngest of all his siblings. They would often be out and about in Baltimore, but Muggsy wasn't that type of person. Muggsy and me, we were either over at each another's house or at the rec center."

3
FAMOUS POETS

I PLAYED ON THE GREATEST HIGH SCHOOL BASKETBALL TEAM IN THE history of the game. There's no doubt about it. We're at the top of all the lists and we know it in our hearts. In 2017 ESPN even made a documentary about us called *Baltimore Boys*. There are a few other contenders, of course, like the 1993 Oak Hill Warriors with the high-flying Jerry Stackhouse or the 1989 St. Anthony's Friars with the floor general coach's son, Bobby Hurley. But really there is no competition for the No. 1 spot. It's us: the Dunbar Poets. Here's why: in my senior year, our 1982–83 team was ranked first in the nation and we went undefeated, 31–0. But to prove that wasn't a fluke, our 1981–82 team went 29–0 the year before. That's a perfect 60–0 for you non-math majors. I never lost a game at Dunbar. During both seasons I was the starting point guard. Those years were some of the best of my life.

I can still remember the day I got my first Dunbar uniform: No. 14. It was the smallest they had. Later, I'd drop the 4 and wear No. 1 in the pros. When I got it, it felt like I'd been waiting my whole life for that Dunbar jersey. It was maroon and gold with white trim, and the day I put it on, my heart raced so fast that it's never stopped. I had a great time at Dunbar. It was unbelievable. I had a lot of friends, I loved my teachers, and the ladies even gave me some nice attention. I didn't have beef with anyone on campus, and our team was quite the draw. Going 60–0 in back-to-back years brings you some pretty hefty attention, especially since those two Dunbar teams produced four first-round NBA draft picks (three of them in 1987). But none of our accomplishments came easily. They all came from years of hard work. All of our success derived from the discipline that our coach, Mr. Robert Wade, instilled in us each and every day. There is no success without sweat.

Today, the name Bob Wade carries undue baggage in the sports world. After our historic back-to-back championship-winning seasons, Coach Wade went on to coach at the University of Maryland, replacing the notorious Lefty Driesell in 1986 after Len Bias died tragically from drug use. After he died there was a cover-up on campus. Because of that Coach Driesell was fired, and Maryland hired Coach Wade, who became the first Black coach of a major sport in the conference's history. But the program didn't put him in a position to succeed, and he left under a dark cloud. I can't say I was surprised with how they treated him, but it's still a shame. At Dunbar Coach Wade had achieved an amazing 341–25 career record. But at Maryland he had some ups and downs, especially at first. The NCAA had gutted the university's scholarships because of the Bias drug scandal, so the team struggled without enough top talent.

Eventually, Coach Wade got the program on track, and Maryland made the NCAA Tournament. But he was later accused of giving small amounts of money and middling assistance to his recruits. He took it on the chin in the press and was forced out of the job. To me, Coach Wade will always be a hero. He is the patron saint of Baltimore basketball. He is a good man through and through, someone everyone knew to respect. Coach Wade always made sure us players kept our heads on straight when we played for Dunbar. He cared about academics, knew what it meant to be a Poet. He'd grown up in the area and survived it. That didn't just go for the starters; it was for all the players on the team. That's why we were so good. Our real competition didn't come in the games. It came in practices. Once we knew what we could do there, we knew we could beat everyone else by any margin we wanted. Coach Wade knew how to handle all our egos, too. He got us to care about one common goal: winning together.

Coach Wade cared about us even after we graduated. Not every coach is like that with his players. He had his little spies everywhere in Baltimore looking out for us to make sure we were okay. If we were someplace we shouldn't be, someone would tell Coach Wade, and he'd get us out of there and take us home. I'll always be grateful for that, and it's one of the many reasons Coach Wade and I are still friends to this day. In many ways his teaching was the turning point for me and my family. He was so good at his job that in 1983 he was named the *USA TODAY* High School Basketball Coach of the Year. Two years before that, though, Coach Wade put bricks in our hands and showed us what hard work was. We did defensive slide drills, wind sprints, and jumping exercises with those damn, heavy red bricks in the palms of our sweaty hands.

We wrapped each of the bricks with duct tape and cloth from old cut-up Dunbar baseball uniforms so they wouldn't slice our hands up, but they were still very heavy. There wasn't a day playing basketball for Coach Wade when I didn't have a brick in my hand. I had nightmares about them. Coach Wade had accepted the men's basketball head coaching job at Dunbar High School in 1975, two years after the former longtime coach, William "Sugar" Cain, retired. Sugar, who had played for the Harlem Globetrotters, won city and state championships for Dunbar. Coach Wade, who took the job as head basketball coach, head football coach, athletic director, and head of physical education when he was hired, was also a former defensive back in the National Football League. He'd played for the famed coach, Vince Lombardi, for a season. Coach Wade said Lombardi's top three priorities were: family, religion, and his profession. Whenever the team had an away game, his family and a priest accompanied them.

As a mentor Coach Wade knew what he was doing. He knew what it took at the highest levels. Coach Wade taught many good players in his day, but he had his eye on my grade from the moment he got the job at Dunbar, even though we were years away from varsity. He knew we had something special as a group. I'd known him from watching Stroh play at Dunbar a few years before me and I liked his demeanor. He was no nonsense but very kind. Once Reggie Williams, Reggie Lewis, David Wingate, and I got to the team, he had us hit the ground running. But Coach Wade was smart. He knew we wouldn't get anywhere without discipline and hard work. And those bricks. The streets of Baltimore are littered with stories of unfulfilled promise. And the streets around Dunbar High School were littered with bricks. Coach Wade didn't want us to just scratch the surface of our possibility. He wanted us to achieve our best.

We played sharp for Coach Wade. We played smart for Coach Wade. If there were any jitters before a game, they were gone by the time we scored our first basket. He'd prepared us to succeed. It was the discipline instilled in us by Coach Wade that carried us through all those victories. We crushed teams in the process. We were fast, we were good shooters, and we were a tight-knit bunch. We fed off each other. We were so good and so deep that Truck was our sixth man during my senior season. The future captain of the Boston Celtics was our sixth man in high school. *Can you believe that?* We actually called our bench the No. 2 team in the country just behind our starters. But the funny thing was just because we knew how good we were doesn't mean the world did—at least not in my first year at Dunbar. To be sure, when I was introduced at the away games, people would laugh. It was like the Lafayette courts all over again. But after I got done with them, their jaws were on the ground. Coach Wade told me that hearing me heckled and ridiculed like that was one of the "lowest" points in his career. He'd take me aside during some games and ask, "Are you okay, Big Fella?" And I'd say, "Yeah, coach. We're about to have a party in here!"

Then we'd proceed to torch the other teams, winning by double digits. When I'd get steal after steal, a team's confidence would start to dwindle. I could always see it in their eyes. After the game, the other team's fans would become our new fans. They cheered as I walked off, victorious. There's one game everyone still talks about during my senior year at DeMatha High School in Washington, D.C. It was one of those games where everyone in the stands thought I couldn't play, but by halftime their mouths and eyes were big circles. At one point in the game, as my energy and adrenaline soared, I came down the lane with the ball and leapt up into the air.

I wasn't sure in that split-second whether I was going to lay the ball in or find a teammate. Then, all of a sudden, I was surrounded in mid-air by two defenders. So I hung in the air a bit longer. I twirled 360 degrees like a ballet dancer and through the smallest opening found Russ with a pass behind my head just as he cut directly to the hoop. He flushed it for a big dunk.

Although it took athleticism and precision to make that pass, it also took our whole lives to grow that mental connection. Russ and I clicked in that instant because of the history we'd built up. Russ slammed the ball, and the crowd erupted. It worked because he knew that if I had the ball and he ran the lane, he'd get the rock in perfect position to score. We had our own language, and in the game of basketball, chemistry is often what wins big games. A team can have all the talent, but if they don't gel, if they don't want to make each other better, then they're not going to win at the highest level.

I'm proud to say Dunbar won at the highest level. In my first year, I was named the MVP of the Baltimore City public school tournament after we won the school's sixth consecutive city championship. I was pretty famous in the city by now, but it wasn't anything like Russ. He was truly a celebrity. Magazines, newspapers, and radio stations in Baltimore and around the country were all talking about him (not to mention the other teams' fans and coaches), wondering what he would do in the NBA, which made me quietly wonder the same thing about myself. People were already predicting Russ to be an NBA lottery pick. By the time we were seniors, our team was ranked first in the nation again. We'd beaten everyone in our path. Some games the experts predicted to be close contests like games with the highly thought-of Camden High School squad in New Jersey, when I was a junior. When we played them, they were the No. 1 team with the No. 1 player, Billy Thompson. I remember Camden's fans laughed as I was introduced. But we just blew them out like everyone else and laughed about the game on the bus ride home.

Losing wasn't in our vocabulary. During our 31–0 senior season, Russ averaged 24 points, 13 rebounds, and four assists. He was a great scorer, but he'd also learned how to pass. I like to think he picked up a few tricks from me. Russ had his pick to go anywhere in the country. He was now the nation's top prospect. Russ threw out enough recruitment letters to start a Dunbar bonfire. In the end, though, he chose to play for Georgetown University and the great John Thompson. Gate was a year older than us and had gone to Georgetown. I remember him telling us it was a tough transition and that Coach Thompson was even harder on his players than Coach Wade. He said the academics were harder, too. There was more pressure. But when Russ decided to join him, Gate got a big smile on his face. He was so excited for the reunion. (The two would win a national championship together.) I admit that I was a little jealous it worked out so well. But I was happy it did, of course. We celebrated Russ with some crab cakes at the harbor.

But I was doing well, too. In between my junior and senior seasons, I'd signed a letter of intent to attend the ACC's Wake Forest University in Winston-Salem, North Carolina, on a full academic scholarship. I wasn't heavily recruited as a junior, even though our Dunbar team was outstanding, and I was the team's leader. But because of my height, coaches weren't sure that I could do it on the Division I level. Nevertheless, I kept working and after my junior season started to attend some important All-Star camps. These were big stops for me, and I encourage any young players out there to attend them if they can. It was at these All-Star camps that I began to make my name on a national level, where I took the next important step forward. At that point I'd had interest from smaller schools like UNC-Charlotte, Drake, and Texas Pan-American. I'd spoken with Seton Hall coach P.J. Carlesimo, who I'd later play for in the pros, and coaches from Virginia and Penn State, too. But nothing seemed like a match.

In the end I wanted to play in the vaunted ACC. That was the conference I knew best, and it had a great basketball reputation with schools like N.C. State and UNC, coached by Jim Valvano and Dean Smith, respectively. But Wake Forest seemed like a great fit from the beginning. It was a good program with a great academic reputation that competed in a top-notch conference against top-notch opponents. I'd visited the campus, and it was smaller than I'd expected. But I knew not to judge that. Compared to Baltimore, it was very different and a universe away. But it was also beautiful on campus. I'd visited as a recruit and saw how historic everything looked. Tradition was everywhere at the school. People said Wake had a very Ivy League feel, which I knew meant old. Even if I didn't feel totally comfortable at first, I knew I'd eventually find my place there. I signed on the dotted line before my senior season at Dunbar thanks largely to those All-Star camps.

In 1982, between my junior and senior year, I was named MVP of the B/C camp in Georgia and the McDonald's Classic in D.C. These were some of the first crucial stepping-stones for me making a national name for myself. People saw that I could hang with the country's top recruits at these camps. But I really got noticed in a major way at Howard Garfinkel's famed Five-Star camp in Pittsburgh. That one attracted famed coaches like Bob Knight, Hubie Brown, and Rick Pitino. I have to thank Coach Wade for that, too. After our undefeated junior season, Coach Wade was invited to work at Garfinkel's camp. His reputation from our teams had earned him some prestigious gigs at camps around the country, including at Five-Star. It helped me to know there was someone at the camp like Coach Wade who knew what I could do, who didn't just know me for my height.

When Coach Wade and the other coaches split up the players for teams at the start of camp, he took me as his top guard to the shock of the other coaches and players, which included big-time stars like Brad Daugherty and Chris Washburn. Coach Wade had a smirk on his face, though, knowing what I could do. Together we upended the camp, going undefeated again. As a result, I caught the eye of Wake Forest assistant coach Ernie Nestor. He sought out Coach Wade and began to get a feel for my game and personality by asking him a few questions. When Coach Nestor got the information he needed, he took the report back to Wake Forest's head coach at the time, Carl Tacy. Coach Tacy just wanted to know one thing: could I play for real? When he found out I could, he was sold. After camp I got a little more attention from schools like Georgetown and Coach Thompson. But nothing substantial materialized.

Coach Thompson, who was one of most highly recognized coaches ever to do it, later told me that he regretted not recruiting me more. Well, I guess we both did all right. It would have been nice to run with Russ and Gate. In fact, Russ told me he'd lobbied Big John to get me to transfer, but John said that if he did, he might lose his job. Sometimes you have to play the hand you're dealt. You have to make your own way. When Coach Nestor first talked with Coach Wade, one of the things they discussed was whether or not I'd have a legit shot to compete for a starting spot at Wake

Forest. Coach Wade wanted to make sure I wasn't getting sweet-talked by the empty promises of a program. He looked Coach Nestor in the eye and asked point blank, and Coach Nestor, to his credit, answered honestly. He said I'd sit much of my first year and have the chance to start after that. So with Coach Wade's blessing, I was officially headed to Wake.

My last game as a high school player came at an All-Star tournament in D.C., where I was again named the MVP. It felt exciting to end my high school career on a high note, even though the thought of never wearing a Dunbar uniform again saddened me. Life, ironically, is too often about endings. But the silver linings are the memories we carry with us after it's all said and done. If our junior year was a success, then our senior year was a triumph, culminating in back-to-back city and state championships and four first-round NBA draft picks. That might never be accomplished ever again. Yet, as always, it wasn't all fun and games. There was real work ahead. When basketball is the focus of your life, when it's all you think about, when it's your love and your career, it's hard not to listen to what other people say about you. You're a public person, and people are constantly talking about where you rank, what your future is.

Heading into Wake Forest, my freshman class included some great point guards from around the country, including the likes of Steve Alford, who went to Indiana University; Mark Jackson, who went to St. John's University; and Pearl Washington, who went to play at Syracuse University. We'd all eventually make it to the NBA and have solid professional careers. They were the players who I liked to measure myself against. Those were the standouts. Yet, at every level of the game, I had to continue to prove myself in ways that other players didn't have to. Because I was different, I always seemed to have to do more than my peers. I'd heard about the Greek myth of Sisyphus by that point, how he had to push the same rock up the same mountain forever, and I felt like I knew what that was like now. But at least I was pushing the rock that I loved most in the world.

Basketball, though, has never been my *entire* life. At Dunbar I'd liked a lot of subjects in school, including math, which was my best subject. A few teachers really helped to inspire me, too. They saw me as more than just a basketball player. When you're an athlete, it can be hard to get your eyes off the game and onto the textbooks. But Dunbar teachers knew I could do more than just play the game. They saw me as more than just a stereotypical dumb jock. They cared about my education. Carolyn Palmer, my math teacher, walked me home after school. She was also a friend of my sister's and thought I was younger than I really was. There were others, too, like Mr. Green, who taught economics; Mr. Cubs, who taught history; Ms. Hawkins, who taught business; and Mrs. Kelso, who taught English.

In a story that still makes me laugh, I'd been on television for a live interview, but I'd messed it all up, speaking garbled and marble-mouthed. I'd been confident going in but froze up once I got on camera. Instead of demeaning me for it, my teacher, Mrs. Kelso, took me aside and taught me how to be a better public speaker. She showed me tricks to remember and how to prepare myself going into an interview. She told me it's just like the game of basketball and that I had to prepare and practice to be excellent. Instead of giving up, I've been good at public speaking ever since, thanks to Mrs. Kelso. That I had teachers and coaches like this has always made me value education. It's something I believe in so seriously that I have considered myself not only a basketball player, but also a teacher of the game throughout my career.

Outside of school I was often with Russ hanging with the guys on the team. We'd joke around, go down to the harbor to get a bite to eat, and talk about girls or our next game. I also spent a lot of time with my brothers but not as much as I wanted, to be honest. I was so wrapped up in basketball. My brother Chuckie was older, so he was exposed to things in the city before I was. Growing up, my brothers and I would often play cards for spare change or candy. But as he got older, Chuckie became more reclusive and more interested in staying out late. He'd started to use drugs in a serious way by about 15 years old. I loved Chuckie, just like I loved Sherron and Stroh. But Chuckie was always the one I worried about most. He had a good heart. But from heroin to cocaine, there also wasn't a drug he didn't like. It can hurt to talk about these things today, to be honest. It's hard to think of your family members strung out, addicted, and in pain.

In my own personal life, I was about to experience another big moment, a major milestone before heading to Wake officially. My girlfriend at the time was pregnant. All of a sudden, I was going to be a father. Was I prepared for that? When she told me the news, thoughts rushed through my mind. Was I ready to be a dad? Family had always been important, but could I really start my own family now? I wasn't sure if I wanted to start a family with my girlfriend. I liked her fine. But in my heart of hearts, I knew I didn't want to marry her. I was young (and broke) and had a career ahead of me that required a lot of attention and sacrifice. My eyes were on college and then hopefully the National Basketball Association.

Amazingly, my mother said she would help take care of the new baby while I was in college. That helped me feel comfortable with the situation. When I think of my mom today, all the MVP trophies and headlines I've ever earned don't amount to a fraction of what she's meant to me. With a support system now in place, our little daughter, Tyisha, was born into the world. She came to us at the end of my senior year at Dunbar. Immediately, I was in love. I knew I would do my best to make everything okay for Tyisha. I would work with her mom so that she could grow up with every advantage we could offer. I saw my future in her sweet little brown eyes. I wanted to be a better person for her. If I ever wanted to quit, I would just think of her. I wanted to show her she could do anything in this life. So I had to go out there and prove it to her first. Now I was ready for Wake Forest. Or so I thought.

MEMORY LANE
Coach Bob Wade

"Muggsy and them thought I was crazy to have them do all those calisthenics with the bricks and run the back stairwell with those bricks. But late in the year, they realized the bricks paid off. Defensively, they were able to have good leg and arm strength, good finger strength, and stamina. When the fourth quarter rolled around in the game, they were catching their second wind. Muggsy griped about it at first, but he knew it was a tradition at Dunbar.

"Where Dunbar was located, they were doing a lot of construction, a lot of urban renewal. They were tearing down a lot of old homes. Dunbar was a stone's throw away from John's Hopkins Hospital, and it was buying a lot of property around the area. It was tearing down homes, and I saw a lot of bricks laying out there. So, I came up with the idea since we didn't have fancy weight equipment where kids could go in and lift weights.

"My trainer and I took a laundry cart and rolled it up the street two blocks from the school and picked up as many bricks as we could. We loaded the laundry cart and rolled them back to Dunbar. Then we had these old flannel baseball uniforms that weren't being used. So we cut them up and wrapped the bricks in the old baseball flannel and put duct tape around them. That was our exercise equipment."

LIFE IN THE ACC

BALTIMORE, MARYLAND, IS ALMOST 400 MILES FROM WINSTON-SALEM, North Carolina. If you don't stop and you drive the speed limit, it takes about six hours each direction. At times, though, it felt like a trip to the moon. The Winston-Salem Wake Forest campus is just about as different as you can get from the Lafayette Court housing projects in Baltimore. There was so much open space, so much grass and quiet out there in the country. (Anywhere outside the city was the country to me.) I could see the stars clearly at night on campus. People drove expensive cars, and most of the student body was made up of White people. The culture shock was real, no matter how hard I tried to fit in. But that extended to the basketball team, too. As usual, seeing me in person had some of my teammates questioning my skills. Some wondered if I was even a player on the team. People are always dubious. But after a few practices, they were sold on what I could do: defend like heck and run the floor. It's the story of my life.

It always takes time for people to believe in me, which makes me have to believe in myself that much more. When you're different, you see the world differently. Your expectations for life are not always the same as the average person's. You're used to people looking at you in ways they don't look at other people. Being a Black athlete from the inner city on the Wake Forest campus proved that to me often. Being shorter than every other player on the team proved it, too. Being one of the shortest players in the country (or in the history of modern Division 1 basketball) proved that even more so. In a way, it's a gift. You're pushed to see the world through a different lens. I wouldn't change my life or who I am for anything. But it has also presented a series of often redundant hurdles that certainly didn't end or begin at Wake Forest University.

Although Wake had a good athletic reputation, it wasn't exactly a historic powerhouse basketball school. It was my hope that we could call ourselves that one day through hard work as a team. I believed in the program I was part of even when it wasn't always easy to. But none of this was a surprise. I'd visited the campus and I knew what to expect from the place. Wake Forest University is nestled in the center of tobacco country in North Carolina. The school, which was founded on a plantation in 1834 just 24 years before the Civil War, first required its students and staff to participate in manual labor for half of each day in the week. In 1942 Wake admitted its first female students. Later in 1946, thanks to large gifts from the Z. Smith Reynolds Foundation, the campus moved full time from its original spot on land north of Raleigh to Winston-Salem, where it resides today.

The university was desegregated in 1962, three years before I was born. I enrolled in the fall of 1983. The school's most famous athletes include the golfer, Arnold Palmer; the football player, Brian Piccolo; and NBA Hall of Famers and my friends, Tim Duncan and Chris Paul. Other notable graduates include a handful of politicians and actors. In truth, though, it's amazing the school has that many important figures because the student body is relatively so small. That just proves that size doesn't always matter when it comes to impact. Today, only about 9,000 students are enrolled on campus at Wake Forest University—compared to about 30,000 at the University of North Carolina. But it was even fewer when I was there as a student-athlete. Yet we always competed and often played well. Today, the basketball program is respected, especially after Duncan and Paul. Notable Wake players in the NBA recently include Al-Farouq Aminu, John Collins, and Jeff Teague.

Before Wake Forest was known as the home of the Demon Deacons, the school's nickname was the Baptists. The university has deep religious roots. It's not always easy to put into words, but when I was on campus, there was a strong sense of tradition around the place—not all of it good, sadly. I loved much of my time at the school, but the truth is: people who looked like me were not always treated well at Wake. Sadly, that's the case for much of American history. When a place doesn't recognize that history in itself, it can insidiously seep into the day-to-day behavior of the staff and students. In fact, there was one very significant moment during my freshman year that almost made me quit the team and leave the university altogether. I'd been accused of cheating on a test that I hadn't even taken. Can you believe that? It felt like a personal attack.

As soon as I found out people on campus thought I'd cheated, I felt unwelcome. People can be prejudiced even when they don't know it, and that proved it. Here's what happened: the team was in the middle of a tough stretch on the schedule, and simultaneously it was the end of the year and time for final exams. I remember how cold it felt outside then and how far away I felt from Baltimore. We were actually having a great season, but I wasn't playing much, and when we got back from a long road trip, I was supposed to take a final exam. But I wasn't prepared for it and I told the professor that prior to the test. He said that I could come and sit for it, but if I really couldn't finish it, I could come back and do it another time. So, I went to class, but I couldn't answer the questions. So, I just handed in a blank piece of paper and knew I'd try again at another time.

I found out later that I'd been accused of cheating on it. But I hadn't even taken it. School officials said they were going to throw me out of the university. At the time, I knew people around campus were saying that I didn't belong at the school. I don't know if it was because I was an athlete, Black, from Baltimore, or all of the above. I almost packed up right there and left. In a clear-headed moment, though, I called my friend Dell Curry to talk it over. When you're a college athlete, it's important to remember that everyone doesn't have your best interest at heart. That's why it's import-ant to lean on your family and friends for support in your darkest hours. Even though we'd only recently just met on a basketball court, Dell was my friend, and I trusted him. We'd met during a tournament when Wake Forest played Virginia Tech earlier in the season.

There was just something about Curry. We just got along well. As he puts it now, "It was friendship at first sight!" In a way, he reminded me of

Reggie Williams. Calm, mild mannered. Just a few days after we'd exchanged numbers, the "cheating" incident happened. I knew they were in need of a lead guard. So, I called him up to see what it might look like if I transferred to Virginia Tech. I told him what had happened with my final exam, how it felt like the school must have resented me for some reason. Curry encouraged me to keep my head up and to fight through it. But he also said I should come play with him at Virginia Tech if I wanted. I really thought about it. He said, "Yeah, come on, man. I know how you can play."

Next I called Coach Wade, who said he would help me transfer if I wanted to. But he also said that there would be troubles wherever I went, and that's the nature of life. Then I called my mom. She advised me to stay at Wake. She was proud when I told her that I would. I had to really grit my teeth for a while after that. I had to compartmentalize my discomfort with the school and my desire to compete every day on the court. I wanted to put my best foot forward, but I felt angry and resentment all around me from some of the other students. Thankfully, the basketball court is a great place to burn off anger or extra energy. That year, we were actually a really good team. We started the season 10–0 until we lost in our next game to Georgia Tech on a last-second, buzzer-beater. We were ranked as high as No. 8 in the country that season. I remember one game playing against the University of North Carolina and the great Michael Jordan. It was my first time I saw him up close. He was already a prolific scorer. He could really fill it up from all over the court.

Jordan, who grew up in Wilmington, North Carolina, was a marvel even back then. That game would be the first of many times Jordan and I would face off against each other on the court over our long careers. But while Jordan was in his third and final year at UNC and a projected top pick in the next NBA draft, I was in my first year trying to prove myself. Coach Tacy had been clear with me when he recruited me. He'd said I'd come in as the backup point guard, but that the following year I'd have a chance to start. I took him for his word, but that didn't make sitting on the bench easier. That first year, though, I was a key bench reserve. When we needed it, I came into the game to jump-start the team with my energy. I'd get a key steal or assist in a frenetic moment. We had a lot of talent, including future NBA players Danny Young, Delaney Rudd, and Kenny Green.

Yet, it was something of a disappointing year for me personally. In truth, I never wanted to come off the bench, though I understood the reasoning behind it. Months before, I'd been a star. Now I was a bench player. But as the year went along, we continued to play well. We even won a few games in the ACC Tournament. Later, we were selected to the prestigious NCAA Tournament. We played our way all the way into the Elite Eight where we were matched up against a loaded University of Houston team. We were big underdogs in that one, facing the seven-footer and future Hall of Famer Hakeem "The Dream" Olajuwon, who was then known as Akeem, and the high-flying dunker and future Hall of Famer Clyde "The Glide" Drexler. Despite being undermanned we took Houston to the brink, but in the end, we lost 68–63. A few games later, Houston went on to lose in the championship game to Georgetown.

When my freshman season concluded, I'd done all right. I'd often felt frustrated at my lack of playing time, but I had to expect that as a freshman. When I did get the chance to play, I'd played well. I finished the season playing in 32 games, averaging 9.8 minutes, 1.7 assists, one steal, and 1.2 points per game. But I knew I could do much more for the team. I'd survived my first season, which not every recruit can say. That would have to be enough. I'd gotten through the bogus cheating accusation and I held my head up high in the end. With all that behind me, I thought I could now get through anything put in front of me. After the year ended, I went home to live in Baltimore. I tried to go home as often as I could, and it felt good to be home for the summer.

Russ, Reggie Lewis, and David Wingate all came back, too, and we hung out and played basketball together like the old days. Wake Forest found me a job in town so I could earn some money while spending time with my new daughter and family. My mom helped with Tyisha, which I appreciated. She split duties with Tyisha's grandmother. I was doing my best, and while it felt very hard, we were getting through. I looked forward to the next season. But little did I know that my first year at Wake would be our only truly successful campaign. Still, I would find out there are more lessons to be learned in loss. During my sophomore year, we actually opened the season strong. Coach Tacy had given me the keys to the team, and I was our starting point guard. I was happy about that and was ready for the responsibility.

We opened the year with a 5–4 record in our first nine games. Then we won seven more right in a row. In one of the games against Georgia Tech, I shut down the future pro and fantastic shooter Mark Price. He was touted as one of the best guards in the country, but on that day, I had the last laugh, holding him to single digits and well below his average. I earned ACC Player of the Week honors for a game against Duke University. We'd beaten them in overtime. I'd locked down their star player, Johnny Dawkins and held him to eight points after he had scored in double figures in 51 consecutive games. But that game against Duke came with some worry for me. Not long before tip-off, the coaches told me about a death threat that the authorities received from a mentally ill man. He'd wrote that if I played against Duke that night, they'd find me "stretched out" at the morgue the next morning. He called me his "sacrificial lamb." I did my best to shrug it off. What else could I do? I wasn't going to hide.

Of course, no one wants to receive a death threat, but the reality of the situation was that I'd seen and heard worse in my years growing up in Baltimore. I'd already been shot and I wasn't going to let some wacko intimidate me. Besides, if I was going to go, it might as well be while playing basketball. Thankfully, I came out of the game unscathed. However, there was one scary moment when I was at the free-throw line about to shoot the ball when I heard someone step on a paper cup that let out a bang. That almost made me jump out of my skin. But I remember seeing my teammates laugh. (Oh, and we won the game.) Later that season we played N.C. State, and I got to meet the great Spud Webb. He was a year ahead of me, but we came into the ACC the same time. Like me, Spud was a shorter guard. He stood 5'7". But he could play with the best of them. His height was never a disadvantage.

These days, Spud and I still get mistaken for each other because we're two of the shortest players ever to succeed in the NBA. But back then he was a star in college, one of the country's most gifted players. Of course, the media made a big deal of us suiting up against one another in a big game. But Spud and I play with such different styles. He's a good floor general, but when you get down to it, he's a scorer. On the other hand, I'm a facilitator first. He can fill it up while I aim for assists. Anyway, in the end, I'm happy to say that we beat N.C. State that day by a bunch of points, but we couldn't get excited about that win for too long. That's when the losing began. After that win we went 2–8, but it felt worse than that. In the ACC Tournament, we lost to UNC and its big-time guard Kenny Smith.

We accepted an invitation to the less-than-prestigious NIT after that loss, but our hearts weren't into it, and we went out in the tournament's first round. It got worse after that, too. After the season there was a big change. Coach Tacy resigned, and Coach Nestor, who'd recruited me, went on to another job. At the same time, many of our players graduated or left for the NBA draft. The future was now very uncertain. Going into my third year, I knew it was going to be an even bigger uphill battle. But I was proud that I'd ended my sophomore campaign well. It boded well for a better junior season. Despite not playing a ton of minutes, I finished the year setting school records in total steals (85) and assists (207). I averaged 6.6 points per game, but I knew that had to go up next year. I also knew I had to get much better if I was going to get noticed by NBA scouts and go on to play at the next level.

When I went back home to Baltimore that summer in 1984 between my sophomore and junior years, I was determined to become a better shooter. I knew I was going to have to carry more of the offensive load as an upper-classman. So I worked on my game as much as I could, shooting constantly in the gym and in the sweltering Baltimore heat. The highlight of that off-season, however, came at a Dunbar game. Each year, the school hosts a reunion game where the varsity team plays some of the alums. But more important than the game, which we won, was that was the day I met my soulmate and future wife, Kim. Before it was Bogues, Kim's last name was

Lee. And to this day, Kim and I have very different recollections of how that first day went. Kim swears she'd never really heard of me until that afternoon's game.

Kim had an uncle who'd gone to Dunbar and followed the team. But Kim says she'd never really heard him talk about me. *Yeah right!* Kim also had a friend who was dating my old teammate, Mike Brown, and she and her friend came to watch Mike play at the Dunbar reunion game. The Poets that year had finished 29–1 and were again named national champions. But my squad beat them in the reunion game 131–128 thanks in part to my late basket as time ticked down. After the game I was introduced to Kim, and as I remember it, she adored me immediately. She told me later that in the stands her friend had said to her, "That's who you're going to date tonight."

But she said she just brushed it all off. I've heard Kim tell people that when we met she thought I was too short or that my head was too big or whatever. But I could see she was into me right away. These days Kim always tells people that I acted so cocky on our first date that she actually left because of it. That still makes me laugh. Still, we kept in touch while I was at school at Wake. At the time Kim lived with her family in Baltimore County outside the city proper. Her family had some money. But I was a city guy, which Kim liked. Kim lived something of a sheltered life. Even she admits that now. Her father was a respected cardiac surgeon at the prestigious Johns Hopkins University. At first, her parents were somewhat skeptical of me. Kim's mom, Gloria Lee, is known for having a sharp tongue when it came to who takes her daughter out, but even she took to me quickly. Gloria actually knew my mom before she even met me. In later years my mom and Kim's mom would sip Brandy Alexanders together after babysitting our kids.

Kim's parents saw that when it got down to it I was a big softy and that I truly loved their daughter very much. So they learned to love me right back. As my junior year progressed at Wake, Kim and I kept in close touch on the phone. Something inside me knew she was the one for me. Kim was special, and I was starting to fall for her even if I didn't know it quite then exactly. Although the idea of settling down was new to me (I wasn't even 20 years old yet), especially because I hadn't had the strongest example of a marriage growing up in my family, I knew I wanted something to continue between us. What that would look like, I didn't quite know at the time. But I had faith I'd find out with her. Life is full of transitions, and I was prepared for whatever would happen next with us.

That season, after Coach Tacy left the team, Wake Forest hired a new head coach, a guy named Bob Staak. He'd previously been successful at Xavier University in Cincinnati, Ohio. In the first conversations I had with Coach Staak before the season began, he told me I was going to have a bigger role on the team. He wanted me to score more and shoot more. My sister, Sherron, had always told me to shoot. And I'd always told her, "Okay, honey. Whatever you say." But I was flattered now that Coach Staak had faith in me. Whatever the team needed, I told him, I'd do my best to provide for the team. He said he wanted to run an up-tempo offense that year, and I had to carry a big part of that responsibility. He wanted to run, to fill it up. "Sure, Coach," I told him. "You got it!"

MEMORY LANE
Spud Webb

"You think *you're* quick, but Muggsy was *unbelievably* quick. You end up going to other players on your team and you're like, 'No, *you* bring the ball up' because can't nobody bring the ball up against Muggsy. He was pesky and all over the place when you'd try to dribble the ball up the court. You always had to respect his game and be aware of where he was at.

"Back then, if you could play, you were going to be on the team. Everybody knew Muggsy could play. If you played in the ACC and dominated the way he did at the point guard position, you knew he was going to have an opportunity in the NBA, too. But at the same time, as shorter players, every night we had to prove ourselves. If we had a bad night, some people would think that we're just too small."

5

GOING FOR GOLD

BEFORE MY JUNIOR SEASON, THE MEDIA PICKED OUR TEAM TO FINISH last in the ACC. That stung. Although I wanted to disagree with the prognosticators, I knew they might actually be right. We had a new coach, a lot of young players, and few experienced upperclassmen other than me. But I was ready for anything that season. Getting through my first two years had helped me stay in control of my expectations. When I'd entered Wake Forest, survival had been my only real goal. But now that I had more experience under my belt, I had new goals: I wanted to thrive and I wanted to win. I had always hoped for a chance at the NBA and I was beginning to think that it was a real possibility. I'd thought about the league my entire life ever since I got my first basketball. It felt like two more years of hard work and I might get to hear my name called at the NBA draft by commissioner David Stern.

Heading into my junior year, our team only had one other player who measured under 6'0". He was a fine but rarely used guard named Clay Dade, who would go on to average fewer than one point, one rebound, and one assist per game that year (love you, Clay). At 5'3", though, I was the team's starting point guard. To me, the world was my oyster when I was on the basketball court. Things, however, didn't go so well for us during my junior season. Despite Coach Staak's wishes to run and gun, we simply couldn't score with most teams. We had too many young guys on the roster, too much inexperience. Our rotation was rough. The team tried its hardest, and I admired our guys for that. But we didn't have much of a chance. We only averaged 59.8 points per game, which was good for 273rd out of 283 teams in the entire country.

We were outscored by an average of 7.5 points per game, which is way too much. We finished 8–21 on the season, 0–14 and last in the conference unfortunately. I remember one game game in particular during that season. We were playing the University of Maryland and the great Len Bias. In an inspired choice, Coach Staak decided to put me on Bias. I was our best defender. But Bias was Reggie Williams' height! When Bias first realized I was checking him, he asked me what the heck I was doing. "Sorry, big fella," I told him. "I got you tonight."

The strategy almost worked, but as with so many games that year, we lost in the end. We had talent, just not enough of it. But we never lacked for heart. Although the team wasn't playing all that great, I was doing pretty well. By the end of the year, I'd gotten my scoring average up to 11.3 points per game, nearly doubling it from the season prior. I was looking to score more but only when it was the best option for the team's success. I got so many steals that I was often wide open for layups. I loved impacting and changing the game on defense. I also averaged 8.4 assists (which was third in the entire nation), 3.1 rebounds, and 3.1 steals (a school record). I would dart in front of my opponent for the ball or snatch it out of their hands from behind after I'd let them pass me. I was blisteringly fast. That year was my best in my career so far. I finished first in the ACC in assists, steals, and minutes played. Anyone who participates in team sports knows, though, it's not about personal success. A season is measured by team wins. But sadly we didn't accumulate many of those.

During the 1985–86 season, I'd contributed almost 50 percent of our team's total points—132 of my field goals combined with 245 assists. That made me the most productive player for his team in the country. What felt better than that, though, was that my fellow Wake Forest players named me the team's MVP, which was a big honor, especially given all I'd gone through to even keep a roster spot early on. Despite our team struggles, word about my game spread around the country. Word got so far that a few weeks after the season, Coach Staak called me into his office and said the U.S. Men's National Basketball Team was interested in me for their squad. He said it was a big deal. At that time I'd never heard of the FIBA World

Championships. Nevertheless, in April of 1986, I hopped on a plane for the tryouts in Colorado Springs to see what they were all about.

I'd never done anything like this before. I wasn't nervous for the competition against the guys, but I had butterflies in my stomach on the plane. I was curious what the future would hold. Would I be playing for my country? I was one of about 50 players vying for a dozen spots on the team. There was a number of great players there, of course, any of whom I'd seen or played against in college and whom I would go on to play against in the pros. We scrimmaged during the tryouts, and I faired pretty well. It felt good to run with guys at the top of their games. I soon found out that I'd played well enough to get through the first round of tryouts. I was selected as one of the finalists for the team, and three weeks later, that meant I had to fly out to the University of Arizona for a 12-day camp to try and make the final cut. During those practices we worked out with U of A coach Lute Olson, who would lead our team. He worked us pretty hard. But the team was loaded. There was so much talent.

There were big name players like Sean Elliott, David Robinson, Charles Smith, and Armen Gilliam, who were future lottery draft picks and standout big guys. There were a bunch of great guards, too, including Mark Jackson, Kenny Smith, Mark Price, Steve Kerr, and Tommy Amaker. I wasn't intimidated to play against anyone, but I did have a lot of respect for these guys. Practices were fierce, intense. The coaches pushed us, and we responded. They wanted to see who wanted it more. The practices reminded me in a way of my earlier Dunbar seasons, playing against so many future pros in one gym. Once we knew what we could do in practice, we knew we could beat everyone we matched up against. I went at the guards, particularly on defense. I wanted to show my best to the coaches. It was healthy competition, and as fate would have it, the coaches offered me a spot on the squad's final lineup.

I'd made the cut. But if going to Wake Forest felt like taking a trip to the moon, then playing overseas at the world championships was like taking a left turn way past Pluto. To begin with, we played exhibition games in Paris and Lyon, France. And we played tournament games in Malaga, Spain. I'd never been to any of these places before. I'd never even really thought about traveling to these cities overseas. Yet, here I was. During the tournament we beat teams from Ivory Coast, West Germany, Italy, China, and Puerto Rico. This was not like suiting up against N.C. State in a November contest. This was country versus country. At first, I didn't play much. I was a bench reserve, much like my freshman year at Wake. Coaches used me as a spark plug to disrupt things when we needed a steal. From high-flyers to rebounders to long-range bombers, we were a deep team and we had a lot of talent. But as the tournament went on, I played more.

One of our marksmen was Kerr, the Arizona guard who was a deadly three-point shooter from any range. But he also carried with him certain wariness when it came to being overseas at that time. Two years prior, Kerr's father, Malcolm, the president of the American University in Beirut, was assassinated for political reasons. It was an international story and an awful one. The tensions abroad hadn't gone down by the time we'd arrived either. We were still very much in the middle of real terrorism overseas. I tried to put it out of my mind as much as I could. I was roommates with Kenny Smith. At night I remember we heard explosions in the distance while staying in Spain. We had armed guards for protection. They had machine guns and they stood outside our rooms. Soldiers with rifles were positioned on the roof of our hotel. We went to sleep as helicopters chopped in the night sky. I'll never forget those nights, falling asleep wondering if the world was going to crumble. Then we had to play a basketball game the next day. Maybe it wasn't that much different than Baltimore.

We tried to keep one another calm during the whole thing, saying to each other that no terrorist cared about a basketball team. Deep down, though, we weren't so sure. Even taking the bus through the street after games, you saw danger mixed with extreme poverty and children begging for money and food. It was brutal. It felt strange rolling past them in our big bus with our U.S.A. warm-ups on. One time, completely by accident, Kenny Smith and I didn't wake up in time for the bus. To punish us, the coaches made us run in the streets of Madrid in our U.S.A. warm-ups like they would have in America. At the time, I didn't know who to fear more—the coaches or the potential terrorists. In our next game, Coach Olson sat me and Kenny, punishing us. But as the team got behind, he put us in, and we brought the squad back. Kenny played well for us the whole tournament. He averaged 14.7 points per game. To go along with that, Charles Smith averaged 15.3, and Robinson averaged 12.9. Kerr also scored double-digits, averaging 10.

In the quarterfinals of the tournament, we played undefeated Yugoslavia. When I got in the game midway through the first half, I defended the team's best player, the late, great Dražen Petrović. He was the talk of European basketball at the time and in the U.S., too, in many ways. That summer the Portland Trail Blazers had picked Petrović in the third round of the 1986 draft at 60th overall. At that time there were so few foreign players in the league. So being selected even that high was an honor for someone born outside the United States. Sadly, Petrović's life was cut short. He died in a traffic accident in 1993 after averaging more than 20 points per game in back-to-back seasons with the New Jersey Nets. In 2002 Petrović was so beloved that he was posthumously inducted in the Basketball Hall of Fame. But during the quarterfinals that summer, he was mine to check.

Before the game the coaches asked if I minded guarding the 6'5" scorer. I told them, "No problem, fellas." By the time the game was over, I'd held dear Petrović to just 12 points or 15 points below his average, and we won 69–60. In the semifinals against Brazil, I had my best game. In the tournament's 10 total games, I'd scored a total of 40 points, but 12 of them came against Brazil. I also had a game-high five steals to go along with four assists that day. We won 96–80. We were now headed for the finals against the Soviets. That game was about as close as it gets. The Soviets boasted one of the best players in the tournament—really, one of the best players in the world—the big and nimble center, Arvydas Sabonis. Despite standing more than 7'0" and weighing more than 300 pounds, Sabonis was one of the best shooting big guys in basketball and one of the game's historic passers. (His son Domantas later grew up to be a great player in the NBA.)

For his career Arvydas only spent a handful of years in the NBA (and those were well after his prime), but for anyone who saw him at the peak of his skill, he was a monster to handle. Similar today to NBA MVP Nikola

Jokic, Arvydas could move a mountain with his big behind but also thread a needle with a bounce pass. The Soviet team smartly played through him, and it was a battle with us the whole game as Arvydas banged bodies down low with our big guys. It was a high-scoring show, too. But in the end, Kenny Smith, who had started the game at guard along with me, hit a late basket to put us up in the final seconds, and we won 87–85. The U.S.A. took home the gold medal that summer, and I've never felt more proud in my life. It was the first time the U.S. had won gold in more than 30 years and the last time a team of non-professionals would ever take home gold for the U.S. We'd won, and I was there to experience it. I'd made the team and I'd worked my way into an important role. In fact, I was on the floor in the closing seconds, guarding my man as he took the last desperate heave. It fell off the mark and the buzzer sounded. I jumped into the air.

I'd become a fan favorite overseas. Just as in high school, summer camps, and college, fans laughed when I first took the court but soon cheered once they saw how I could play. I brought something special to the tournament that no one had ever seen before. I'd brought selflessness and an attention to detail on defense. But I'd done it at a size no one in Europe had ever seen before on that level. It made me stand out on one of the biggest stages possible despite being the smallest player in the gym. Most importantly, NBA scouts got to see me play against NBA-level talent like Arvydas, Petrović, and all of the other highly-touted players on the teams, including my own. I'd started the final game, and that earned the approval of my peers and the U.S.A. coaches. Basketball was huge for me. But while some of my teammates were headed off to the pros, I had one more year to prove myself at Wake Forest before I could think seriously about an NBA roster.

As my senior year at Wake began, I was ready for my toughest challenge. This was the era when most players stayed all four years—way before the modern one and done. No longer was I an upstart or underdog trying to make an impression. I was a tried-and-true senior, a gold medalist expected to lead the team with poise. To start the year, the school put me on the cover of the 1986–87 media guide. It was an honor. I'd progressed from averaging one point per game and not knowing if I'd even stay all four years to earning the cover of the yearly guide. That's something to puff your chest out about in the bedroom mirror. During my senior season, I was the only person under 6'0" on the team. But that didn't matter much to me, of course. I was our leader and best player. More importantly, it was my responsibility to get the most of out of our guys from possession to possession. It fell on me. Coach used to get on me for going too hard at the young guys in practice. But I only had one gear and I wasn't going to take it easy on anyone.

Unfortunately, just like the year before, though everyone tried their best, our combined talent just wasn't there. As a group we were marginally better than the year before. We finished the regular season with a 14–15 overall record. But we went 2–12 in the ACC. Our only two in-conference wins came against the struggling University of Maryland coached by my old friend, Bob Wade. They were hurting worse than we were. That year we finished seventh in the ACC, only ahead of Coach Wade's decimated, scholarship-less Maryland team. For the season we'd upped our average scoring per game by about 10 points, finishing at 68.9 per contest. That was progress. In the end, though, it was a disappointing regular season for our team, to be sure. The highlight of the year came for us in the annual ACC Tournament. We were such a low seed that we weren't expected to do much. But sometimes that's just when you can play your best.

In the ACC Tournament, we took out the higher-seeded Clemson University team in our first game. They had the conference's Player of the Year, Horace Grant, at power forward. He, of course, would go on to win three championships with Michael Jordan and Scottie Pippen with the Chicago Bulls before playing with Shaquille O'Neal and Penny Hardaway and the Orlando Magic in the mid-1990s. But that day I wasn't going to let us lose. I ran up and down the court, stealing the ball, hitting my teammates with passes, and knocking down shots. We beat Clemson convincingly and moved on to the next round. Next up we played the higher-seeded N.C. State in the semifinals. We took them to two overtimes, pushing the talented team. But I was determined to keep us in the game. Before the second overtime, I squared up and hit a long-distance shot that *I thought* was a three-pointer, but the referee called it a two. I was confident taking the last-second shot. My jumper had improved a lot over the past few years, and seeing it go in was proof of all the work. The shot tied the game and kept us alive.

Later in the second overtime, I took what I thought was a charge in the lane, but the ref called it a block. I'd fouled out of the game with only a few seconds left. We lost, just barely missing a chance to play UNC and Dean Smith in the tournament final. Suddenly, I realized my senior season and college career were over. I was a mix of emotions. I'd wanted to accomplish more as a team, but we just didn't have the talent as a group. But before leaving for good, I found out I was named to first-team All-ACC Tournament. I was the leading vote getter. I couldn't believe it. Usually, your team has to make the final to get recognition like that. But I had despite that. With that on my resume, I began to accept the end of my playing days at Wake. I finished my senior year with an ACC-record 781 career assists and 275 steals. That season I'd also upped my scoring to 14.8 points per game (tops on the team). I shot 50 percent from the field and 81 percent from the foul line. I also averaged 9.5 assists, 3.8 rebounds, and 2.4 steals per game. I'm still the school's all-time leader in steals and assists.

I was named first-team All-ACC. I was also given the Frances Pomeroy Naismith Award for the nation's best player under 6'0" tall. (Coach Smith used to say, "If you can't see Muggsy, pick the ball up!") Wake Forest retired my No. 14 and bestowed upon me its annual Arnold Palmer Award for the school's best athlete. (In 2001 I was inducted into the school's Hall of Fame.) While we didn't accomplish all the goals we'd set out to achieve, we'd worked hard and done our absolute best. I'd made my mark at school and on the national stage. There were many more highs than lows. It had been a challenge, it had been eye-opening. But in the end, it was good. I'd set seven school records, and my chances of making the NBA were strong. Off the court, I thought I had things pretty well figured out, too. But I've often learned in my years that just when thing are going well, that means something is about to go for a big left turn. Sadly, this was one of those cases. Near the end of my academic year, a professor accused me of receiving too much help from a tutor on one of my term papers. He said the essay didn't contain any spelling or grammatical mistakes, so it must not have been honest work from me.

They were trying to paint me as a bad guy yet again. Why? I'll never know. When I heard that, I wondered why the school had even allowed me a tutor. But, of course, it wasn't actually about a tutor or a term paper. It was about prejudice. I found out from my advisor at the time, Gil McGregor, who I will forever appreciate, that the accusing professor wasn't the only person to think I didn't belong at Wake or who thought I was a cheater. McGregor had heard people say a person like me never belonged at Wake Forest. He used that information to clear my name. McGregor helped me fight the charge, and it was later dropped. How can people be so biased toward others? So ignorant? Moreover, how can they cheer me on the court and deride me off of it? That year I left school just shy of a few credits from official graduation. But I promised my mom that I would go back to finish. To my word, I did just that.

But life's surprises didn't end there with my leaving Wake Forest University. Throughout the season I'd stayed in contact with Kim, talking often on the phone. We'd gotten pretty close. When I'd gone home to Baltimore to visit my family throughout the season, I'd always planned to see her. I liked talking with her, seeing her. We were falling in love with each other. But we weren't officially engaged, so I was still sort of playing the field with other ladies on campus. I probably shouldn't have been; I know it was immature. But at the time, I figured why not. I was young, I liked going out with friends. What could a little dancing hurt? Though I hardly ever drank, I liked to party and dance. But I shake my head at myself now, thinking how silly I was. Of course, one day that lifestyle bit me in the butt when Kim decided to surprise me with a visit.

At the time Kim had a close friend who was home from college. So Kim lied to her parents and told them she was going to visit that friend for the weekend and sleep there. But instead Kim flew down to visit me! It was the first time Kim had ever lied to her parents (sorry, Mr. and Mrs. Lee) and the first time she'd ever flown in a plane. But when she got there, I wasn't the best host. With her surprise arrival, I suddenly had to put pictures of her up around my dorm along with the notes and stuffed animals she'd sent me over the years. My roommate even blurted out when she got there, "Where did all this stuff come from, Muggs?" Kim, sitting with me in my dorm, shouted out, "Busted!"

I admit it. I wasn't very slick. I kept turning the switch on the back of the phone off so it wouldn't ring. I didn't want girls to call and for Kim to hear it. Eventually, Kim just said, "Do you think I'm stupid?"

She started to leave, but I began talking sweet—so sweetly in fact that we went all the way that night together. Kim ended up leaving in a huff the next day, angry at all the phone calls I had to silence. I felt really bad about that. Deep down, I knew I was getting too old to try and act like that. That's the stuff that teenagers do. The single life is fun, but at the end of the day, there isn't that extra support and love you need that family can give you. The next day I called Kim, and we began to work it out. I told her I was very sorry, that I would tell anyone else I was talking to that I was seeing someone exclusively. She'd stormed out the day after we'd slept together, but I didn't want her to go. I didn't want to hurt her. I told her I wanted to be a one-woman man from now on and I truly meant it.

It was good that I did, too. Because two months later, Kim found out she was pregnant from the night we'd spent together at Wake Forest after she'd almost stormed out. The baby would be our first child. Kim's parents, of course, weren't thrilled at the idea of their 19-year-old daughter getting pregnant with a college basketball player. They wondered how it had happened since Kim had lied about going to see me. To explain it, we said that I'd come home a few months prior to visit my family. That little lie aside, we were set on having a baby together. We were in love. It was scary, but we felt confident we could do it together—even if her parents were fearful.

If I made it to the NBA like I thought I could, I'd be able to provide well for our family. All my hard work could really pay off. But before that could happen, Kim went into labor on a game night near the end of my senior season. We were playing our rival, Georgia Tech. Kim told me to go play. But after the game, I rushed to call the hospital for an update. They said Kim was in labor and that she couldn't speak. She was exhausted, too.

The nurse told me Kim's parents were with her and that her father, a doctor, was her coach. They were doing well. Kim's dad put ChapStick on her lips and held her hand throughout the whole thing. She went into labor on a Saturday afternoon in 1987, and on Sunday our little Brittney was born. I knew Brittney would be so special. I knew she would change my life.

MEMORY LANE
Dick Vitale

"They listed him at 5'3", but he's really like 5'2". To play in the NBA and achieve what he did, I don't know if he even realizes how special it is. You think a kid that's 5'3" in high school somewhere, you think he's hearing, 'You can be in the NBA?' No, they're laughing at him. They're saying, 'Are you kidding me? You're wasting your time!' But man did Muggsy prove them wrong. He played 14 years in the league at 5'2" or 5'3". That's unbelievable! What an inspiration! People ask me what the chances are of seeing another Muggsy Bogues? I don't think I'll see it in my lifetime."

THE 1987
NBA DRAFT

FAMILY HAS ALWAYS BEEN IMPORTANT FOR ME. FAMILY IS THE FIRST AND last thing I think about when I wake up and put my head down to sleep. If you don't invest in family, something important is likely missing. But family isn't just those to whom you're blood-related. Chosen family is equally important. I've always looked for family wherever I've played. I want my team to feel like one. Chemistry on a basketball team is almost always more important than gradations of talent. The pieces have to fit, and sometimes that takes hard work and attention to detail. Maybe it's because I know what a good family can feel like and I also know what a broken one can feel like, too. But the idea of togetherness has always been central. That's what drew me to *The Bowery Boys* when I was a kid. That's what fueled Sherron and me shooting on the milk crates in the cold. That's what made that 360-degree pass to Reggie Williams at Dunbar High School. Family.

After I left Wake Forest, I went home to Baltimore. Much of my family was around the city except for my brother Stroh, who was stationed at Fort Hood, Texas, with the army. It was the summer of 1987, and my little girl, Tyisha, was living with her grandmother outside the city. She was four years old now. Unfortunately, her mother was dealing with some personal issues, but little Tyisha was in good hands with her grandmother. Along with my mom, Sherron helped to raise her, too. At Wake Forest I'd sent what little money home I could and stayed in touch with Tyisha every day. I promised myself to stay close with and supportive of her, to do whatever I could to help her as she grew up. Even though her mom and I weren't together, I wanted to be in her life as much as I could.

When you ask her, Kim says our daughter Brittney looked exactly like me when she was born with a big head and little legs. She joked, "I went through all that just to get me a mini-Muggsy?" But we, of course, all loved Brittney to the stars and back. I spent as much time with her as I could after she was born. I knew she was going to be a special person when she grew up. But I also had a job to do. It was a busy time then. I had just finished my senior year at Wake Forest and was looking ahead to that summer's NBA draft. I had to do everything I could to improve my draft stock in time, to impress teams and scouts. The higher you're picked in the draft, the more money you can make. But more than that, I just wanted to hear my name called.

Kim and Brittney were home in Baltimore, staying with Kim's parents in the country. But I knew they would soon come to live with me after the draft. Wherever I went in my career, Kim and Brittney would be with me. They were now my foundation. My mom was still working in Baltimore and living in the Lafayette Court housing projects. I wanted to buy her a new home when I made it to the pros. Sherron was working for the city's parks department, and my brother Chuckie was staying afloat, living with them. Drugs and addiction are a tough thing to navigate when it comes to your family. You want to help, but sometimes help isn't what a person wants. I just tried to always stay available. My dad was still in prison. He'd done almost half his time, and I was beginning to form a plan with a lawyer to get him out. I'd learned a thing or two about the power of lawyers at Wake.

Once I had some money, I'd get one to reduce the sentence. Most of all, though, I had to focus on basketball and I knew that meant proving myself at the next level to everyone all over again. None of what I wanted to happen with my family could happen if I didn't continue to work on my game and show what I could do on the court for an NBA scout or seven. My next move was to attend the NBA tryouts. I had to be where the scouts were and I had to impress them. At Wake Forest, Coach Staak told me that no matter how much I'd done in college, those camps would largely determine my future in the league. My ACC and Wake Forest records would only get me in the door and not outright get me drafted. Not only did I have to prove that I belonged, but I also had to get over the hurdle in each scout's mind that someone who was 5'3" would be unable to make a career in the league.

I had to go beyond the box score and impact a given game immensely to show I belonged. Before the tryout camps began, I played in the annual NCAA All-Star Game, which was held during the Final Four in New Orleans that year. Thanks to a solid performance there, I was invited to the Portsmouth NBA camp in Norfolk, Virginia, which was right around the corner. As I began to understand how the tryout system worked, I found out that a lot of big-name players skipped these early camps, thinking they already had a top spot made in the shade. But that can hurt you, too. You can slip in the draft if coaches and scouts don't think they know enough about you as a person, if they think you ducked a workout. I moved the other way, though. I *wanted* to play wherever I could. I wanted to bolster my name and impress everyone who laid eyes on me.

In Norfolk, people were shocked at what I could do both offensively and defensively. I guess they hadn't seen me in the ACC (or cared to pay attention), but as I jetted up and down the court, shutting down the better-known guards, I impressed a lot of guys holding clipboards and whistles. Some days when I was at these camps, I'd think of my sister, Sherron. At Dunbar, she was always yelling from the bleachers for me to shoot, shoot, shoot. Ever since we were little, she's always been telling me to shoot the ball. Sometimes I'd smile for just a moment if I made a shot in a tryout. I can still hear her now, "Shoot! Shoot! Muggsy, shoot the darn ball!" And I'd say, "Yes, honey. Thank you, coach!" She was my biggest fan. I raised enough eyebrows at Norfolk that I was then invited to the more prestigious tryout in Chicago. It was the most important pre-draft workout prior to the NBA draft.

I had to impress the top scouts in Chicago. It was the only thing I could think about. In fact, the head of NBA scouting services, Marty Blake, said I'd personally wowed him in Norfolk and that he'd made sure I was invited to Chicago. He said he knew that I belonged. That was big for me. Chicago was a four-day affair. Fifty-five seniors were invited to try out. It was a huge deal and could make or break my chances in the NBA. Back then, most of the top picks were upperclassmen. We were all there trying to improve our stock, trying to impress the right coach or front office. At the start of camp, I was paired up on a team with the lanky, skilled player named Scottie Pippen. Like Horace Grant, Pippen would later go on to star and win championships with Michael Jordan on the Chicago Bulls. But at this camp, he was like me: a lesser-known guy.

Before camp Pippen, who played at University of Central Arkansas, was projected to be a late first-round pick, and I was projected to go somewhere in the second round. But together we tore the camp up. I still laugh about it now. No one saw us coming. We went undefeated over the entire weekend. Coaches and players kept looking at us, wondering who the heck we were and why we were kicking their more highly-ranked butts. If someone meets me for the first time at a basketball camp, they're not thinking that I've been asked a million times about how tall I am (5'3"), how high I can jump (44½"), if I can dunk a basketball (my hand isn't big enough to grip the ball, but I can tip it in on a rebound), or where that scar on my arm came from (a gunshot). But when you're a 5'3" 145-pound blur, first stealing the ball and then quickly throwing an alley-oop to Pippen, you create some serious curiosity in people's minds.

Pippen and I worked that place. As much as basketball was pressure-packed for me at that time, it was also an escape. I could put everything out of my mind and just play. Nevertheless, real life was always right outside the gymnasium. I'd signed with the well-known and respected agent, David Falk (who I stayed with my whole career). Among other clients, he represented Jordan. I figured I couldn't go wrong with that one, right? Jordan was doing pretty well for himself, after all! After the Chicago camp, my agent told me that scouts were now projecting me in the first round, maybe even in the top dozen picks. I tried not to count my chickens before they were hatched, but I was getting excited about my future in the league. There was some talk that the Utah Jazz were interested in picking me to back up their All-Star guard, John Stockton. Or maybe the New York Knicks, Denver Nuggets, or Dallas Mavericks would bring me in as a starter.

I took the prerequisite physicals for all of these teams, wondering who might get me. Once the rigors of the pre-draft process had concluded, to take my mind off my future, I found ways to make some money. I was no longer restricted by the NCAA amateur status because I was headed to the pros. So, I looked for ways my game could bring in some bucks. At the time, it was *en vogue* to play in summer league tours against a mix of players from a mix of backgrounds. At first, I played with a touring group of ACC graduated seniors, playing against other recent collegiate graduates. We made upwards of $1,000 per week. Next, I played in the United States Basketball League for the Rhode Island Gulls. Spud Webb and Manute Bol had played for the Gulls before their respective NBA teams selected them.

It was the perfect place to keep my game sharp and to make money for my family. In the USBL I went up against the all-world women's basketball player, Nancy Lieberman, who could really hoop. I also played against Micheal Ray Richardson, a prolific scorer who never quite got his career on track while playing in the NBA. But he and other former greats like World B. Free were big helps and mentors that summer, encouraging me and giving me pointers each day. Hearing them tell me I had what it took to make the league and stay there was important that summer. These were former big-time scorers in the league. Even if their games had slipped some since then, they knew what they were talking about. In the USBL I averaged 22.2 points (see, I told you I could score) and 8.4 assists per game. Then, after the quick season, it was time for the NBA draft.

The draft was held on June 22, 1987. The league had invited about 20 guys to attend the draft in person. Russ and me were two of those invitees. At first, people didn't think I would go in the first round. But I kept proving people wrong. Everyone in my family hoped for it, but no one around the world really believed it but me and a few of my peers. I arrived in New York City from Baltimore on the day of the draft. I met up with Russ, Reggie Lewis, and the guys and we went to Madison Square Garden together to see how everything would unfold. We were hyped, but we didn't want to jinx anything. I just kept thinking, *Look at us! Lifelong friends about to achieve our dreams! What could be better!* No high school team had ever had three first-round draft picks in one NBA draft. But Dunbar was about to achieve history that evening. That was special.

When the day began, the San Antonio Spurs were on the clock. With the first pick in the draft, the Spurs selected future Hall of Famer David Robinson, a 7'1" center out of Navy. Robinson was beyond talented and in perfect shape to play basketball. He was the no-brainer first choice for San Antonio. After Robinson went, though, I started to wonder where Russ would be selected. Some people picked him to go as high as second. But with the second pick, the Phoenix Suns chose scoring power forward Armen Gilliam out of UNLV. Next was small forward/shooting guard Dennis Hopson to the New Jersey Nets. With the fourth pick, the Los Angeles Clippers selected my best friend Russ, and I was so happy for him. He'd done it! All that hard work paid off. Russ took the stage with a smile, and I thought, *Look at my guy!* He'd earned every bit of it. He was onto more great things. With the fifth pick, Pippen went to Chicago (via a trade with the Seattle SuperSonics).

Guards Kenny Smith went sixth to the Sacramento Kings, and Kevin Johnson went seventh to the Cleveland Cavaliers. At some point, I was sitting next to my buddy Mark Jackson, another point guard who, like me, liked to pass. Jackson played at St. John's University and was a standout there, for sure. We kept wondering where the other one would go. I kept joking, "Where we going to go, honey?" I had a tendency to call people "honey." I don't know why. I've just always done it as a joke for myself. I told Mark that I'd heard the Knicks were interested in me, and he said the Washington Bullets were interested in him. Right then, we proposed a fake trade with those two teams. I could play near Baltimore in Washington D.C., and he could play in his hometown of New York. Who figured that it could potentially work out so perfectly. In the meantime I looked up to the big draft board and realized everything had been moving so fast!

Horace Grant went 10th to the Bulls and the sharp-shooting Reggie Miller went 11th to the Indiana Pacers. Then, legendary NBA commissioner David Stern took the podium. He held the envelope and began to speak. "With the 12th pick in the 1987 NBA draft…" I held onto every word. They hung in the air like balloons. "The Washington Bullets select…" I listened like he was telling me the greatest secret. "Tyrone Bogues from Wake Forest University!" *Boom! I'd done it!* My smile couldn't have been wider. Kim told me that my whole family, watching together on TV, screamed when they heard my name get called. They woke up little Brittney with their shouting. I was a first rounder! And I knew I could take care of my family's future if I kept my head on straight. It was a humbling experience and one I'll certainly never forget.

I walked onto the stage, completely elated. My selection was notable in that I was the only player shorter than the commissioner that night. I shook Stern's hand and smiled as big as I could for our photo together. It was like commencement for us college players. He congratulated me, and I thanked him. I stepped off the stage and got my Bullets hat. I put it on before I went to do some press obligations next. It felt serendipitous and ironic to be chosen by a team named "The Bullets" after getting shot at five years old. That buckshot changed my life, gave me a surreal dose of confidence. Now, here I was. After a few interviews, I joined Russ backstage, and we jumped for joy together. We'd made our dreams come true, becoming top 12 picks! It was an indescribable feeling of relief and happiness, even though we knew we had a lot of work to do ahead of us next season.

The draft continued, and I heard the Knicks select Jackson with the 18th pick (he'd go on to win Rookie of the Year that season). Later, the Boston Celtics picked Truck with the 22nd pick. Truck had done really well in his senior season at Northeastern University in Beantown. He'd blossomed into one of the nation's top scorers and defenders. He was the team leader and earned them win after win. He'd also shot up taller since high school. He was about 6'6", the perfect size for a shooting guard. The Celtics had an up-close look at him at Northeastern in Boston and they knew what they were getting with him as a player. With his selection Dunbar had officially made NBA draft history. Russ, Gate, Truck, and me had all made the league. Three for three. With Gate drafted the year before, we'd really done something big. Since us, more great Baltimore players have made the league like Carmelo Anthony and Sam Cassell. But I'm proud to say that we helped that trend in a big way in 1987.

After the draft that day, Russ and I flew back home to Baltimore. Everyone was going crazy for us in the airport, cheering us on like we were returning from battle. I found out Stroh had been able to listen to the draft on the radio in Fort Worth, Texas. To celebrate it, we partied through the night. It was fantastic! But there was another side to it. I didn't know it at the time, but Kim and my mom were secretly worried. They'd hoped any other team in the league other than the Bullets would select me. They didn't want me close to home, close to potential distractions. When Kim told me that, I made sure to listen. I knew the most important thing in my life beside my family was my relationship to basketball. My family's advice was important to me. The streets are lined with stories of *almosts*. I wasn't going to add another to it.

I wasn't going to be one of those. I was going to use my brain and my talent to make something of myself for the sake of my family. Needless to say, I was excited for the start of the new season. The Bullets were a historic NBA franchise. The team won the NBA championship in 1978 with two of the all-time greats: Elvin Hayes and Wes Unseld. The Bullets had gone to the Finals the following season, too, but lost to Seattle, who they'd beaten the year before. Since the late '70s, the team had remained solid but not anything stellar. The franchise hovered around .500 most seasons but hadn't made a deep playoff run since those back-to-back Finals appearances. But I was hoping to be part of the team that changed all that. I envisioned myself running the squad, handing out dimes on the break to legends.

Over the summer my agent had worked on my contract. In the meantime with the money I'd made in the various summer leagues, Kim and I found a place to stay in Washington. While I loved living with both Kim and our daughter, it did take a bit of time getting used to being with them 24 hours a day. I wasn't used to the domestic life, to be totally honest. I'd never settled down before. It wasn't like I was trying to date other people. I just wasn't used to living with other people. Ultimately, it was what I wanted. Kim and I haggled over budgets, furniture, raising Brittney. But that's what young couples do until they figure it out. We did our best to make it work smoothly. We were committed. It was important for me to be unified for Brittney as she grew up. I knew that wasn't possible with Tyisha's mother, but I wanted to do what I could for Brittney.

Before I officially signed my contract with the Bullets, the team held a press conference to introduce me as their top pick to the local media. Although the idea of it brought a smile to my face, the press conference itself made me roll my eyes more than Vegas dice on a craps table. I was introduced to the press by then-senator Chic Hecht of Nevada, who was then the shortest male senator at 5'5". There were enough short jokes during the press conference to make you sick. I grinned through it, though, like a good soldier. After that I went back home with Kim and Brittney and waited for my agent to finalize my deal. This was before the standard rookie scale contracts of today, and as a result, the whole process took a lot longer than I liked. It went down all the way to the wire. I didn't want to miss a moment of training camp or a single game.

Thankfully, my agent got it done, and I was set to start. He'd negotiated a $1 million contract over four years. It was the kind of money I didn't even know how to dream about. Immediately, I had a few things to check off my list. First, I bought myself a new Mercedes-Benz. Then I made plans to buy my mom her own house. At first, she didn't want to move away from the Lafayette projects, but once she did, she was so happy to have her own home and her own green lawn. Sherron and my brothers moved into the new house with her. It was located in Ellicott City in Howard County in Maryland. We were one of the first families to move into that neighborhood before a whole community quickly sprouted up around us. I also began an endorsement deal with a local Ford dealership, promoting their—of course—small Ford Fiestas. It was fitting, so to speak. But before the season started, I had one more thing on my list to finish.

My father was still serving his sentence in prison. I knew I had to help get him out. For armed robbery, my father served a dozen years and had more on the way. But I hired an attorney and just like that, he was free. It was 1988, and my father was a free man. I wondered how he would adjust.

I couldn't imagine how difficult that might be. Amongst his cellmates, he'd been a respected citizen inside. He was a basketball coach, and the guys gave him props because his son was a big-time player. While he was inside, my mom had visited him every week. Somehow, she had the strength. He was inside but a piece of her was, too. Not a Saturday went by without a visit from her. A few weeks after he got home, my parents got to attend one of my first preseason games in the NBA. They sat in the stands together to watch me. It was the first time my dad had ever seen me play. It brought tears to my eyes.

MEMORY LANE
Mark Jackson

"Sitting at the draft knowing at the time the Washington Bullets needed a point guard and that not so many of us were left on the board, they selected Muggsy, and obviously it was frustrating from my standpoint! But at the same time, I understood just how special of a talent he was. It was a credit to his greatness. Everybody understood how awesome of a player Muggsy was and how he impacted the game. He was a nightmare to play. It became something you expected when you faced him in the league."

7

FROM THE BELTWAY TO THE QUEEN CITY

DURING MY FIRST TRAINING CAMP WITH THE WASHINGTON BULLETS, I MET some of the NBA's all-time legends, including the big center and future Hall of Famer Moses Malone. Growing up, if you followed basketball at all, it was impossible not to hear about Malone. He was an all-time great even before he retired. A three-time MVP, Malone was one of the league's best scorers and rebounders. He was a double-double machine and the first player ever to enter the pros straight out of high school. The ABA's Utah Stars drafted Malone in 1974. Later, he won the 1983 NBA championship on the Philadelphia 76ers with Julius "Dr. J" Erving. I also met Jeff Malone (no relation to Moses). He was a talented shooting guard and an All-Star the year prior. Bernard King, the great scorer, was on the team, too. He quickly became a good friend. He had stories from the league's early days when it wasn't in as good a financial shape as it is now. Another person I clicked with was our 7'7" Sudanese center Manute Bol. Like me, Manute garnered a lot of attention because of his size.

People always wanted to pair Bol and me in photos. I never really liked that since it was only because of our height and not necessarily because of our games. I knew I could play and I knew Bol was a skilled big man who could shoot from the outside. Bol quickly became a close friend despite our awkward press requirements. He used to tell me he'd killed lions with spears in the Sudan. We spent a lot of time talking together. He'd come into the league two years before and offered advice to me as I was trying to find my way. Bol helped to make a rocky season a little less so. Our team had a lot of talent. The trick was fitting it all together at the right times and finding someone who could run the show. I thought that would be me. But it quickly turned out not to be the case. At the time the coach of the Bullets was Wes Unseld. In his playing days, Unseld was one of the best big men ever to do it. An imposing, bruising center, he was an NBA MVP in 1969 and Finals MVP in 1978. In college he'd averaged 20.6 points per game and 18.9 rebounds. Staggering numbers!

But I couldn't stand him as a coach. The coach/point guard relationship should be sacred. The two have to be in unison for the team to go anywhere. But Unseld and I weren't. It was too bad because if I'd ever played with him, I'd have been sure to get him the ball first thing. Unseld had been an executive with the Bullets after he'd retired as the franchise's best player. That's the role he had when I was drafted. But he came down from the front office to coach the final 55 games of my rookie season. Prior to his arrival as coach in 1988, I'd started the first few preseason games under then-coach Kevin Loughery. In my first preseason game, I'd played against the great Detroit Pistons point guard Isiah Thomas. I only scored one basket that game, but it was from a steal I got off Thomas. I picked his pocket and then took the ball to the other side of the court. Then I saw the big forward Rick Mahorn at the rim. I pulled up for a jumper, and thankfully it went in.

We also played in the preseason against Magic Johnson and the Los Angeles Lakers. Before that game Magic told me, "Welcome to the league." It felt surreal to be known by Magic. After the game he compared me to a fly buzzing around his face. It was funny; I could feel myself begin to make my name in the league. People who I'd looked up to were now learning about me. But Unseld didn't much care. During the regular season, we got off to a slow start. I did, too, unfortunately. I started in the team's first game against the Atlanta Hawks and led us in assists. But as the season progressed, I started to force passes that I normally wouldn't even attempt. Uncharacteristically, I turned the ball over. I was trying too hard and subsequently getting mad at myself for doing so and for hurting the team. Before I knew it, Coach Loughery got the axe, and Unseld came down from the front office. Like so many others, Unseld couldn't see past my height. On top of that, he wanted to play slow. The funny thing was, though, despite not respecting my game, he had to keep playing me. I was a spot starter on the team then because we'd incurred so many injuries throughout the first half of the season.

Players kept going down, so I was the lead guard by default under Unseld. Yet, there was always talk of him benching me. By December my game started to slip amidst all the uncertainty and transitions. One of my only highlights that year was when I hit a one-handed half-court buzzer-beater (one of a few I'd make over my career). The fans loved that one, and I still see it run on highlight reels every now and then. That season the only things that kept me going on the court were the relationships I had with my teammates, guys like King, the Malones, and Bol. Those guys were like big brothers to me during my rookie season. Moses had seen it all. He was a vet's vet. He didn't talk much, but when he did, you knew to listen. I remember hearing a story about how Charles Barkley once went to Moses Malone to ask him why he wasn't playing on the 76ers in the mid-1980s. Moses was plain with Chuck: "You're too fat and you're lazy." Immediately, Barkley dropped like 50 pounds and became and all-time great.

Throughout my first year in the league, Moses just told me to keep working and to ignore the politics of the NBA. He told me to ignore what I couldn't control. But one occasion that really bugged me that year was when *The Washington Post's* sports columnist, Tony Kornheiser, called Bol and me the team's circus show. Why don't they arrive in a "clown car?" he wrote. That was an especially low point for me that season. I knew it was a joke, but why make it? By the end of the year, I wasn't playing much at all. Honestly, I was ready to get away from the team as fast as possible. It felt like a wasted season. All I'd learned was how harsh the NBA could be. On the court, I'd done all right. I'd played in 79 games, starting 14 of them, averaging 20.6 minutes. I'd notched 5.0 points, 1.6 steals, and 5.1 assists per game (tops for the team). Statistically, it wasn't bad, but I considered the whole year a bust. I'd made the league, but it was basically all downhill from there. People were still looking at me as just a 5'3" player, a gimmick to sell tickets at best.

I was learning quickly that the NBA could be a tough ecosystem. I'd achieved the top of my profession and still there were many doubters. But thanks to my guys on the team, I pressed on. I knew that if I ever got to be a veteran in the NBA, I would be the kind of guy to help younger players, to give them advice. Teaching is such a vital part of the game. I'd learned that early in Baltimore under people like Mr. Howard and Coach Wade. That year in Washington, we finished the season with a 38–44 record and made the playoffs as the seventh seed. We were pitted against the second-seeded Pistons. It ended up being a close series, but we lost to them in five games. When it was over, I was glad for it to be done, to be honest. After the season Unseld brought me in his office and said that he planned for me to be the starting point guard next season. He said he was going to bring me back and put the ball in my hands. But I didn't believe him.

Unfortunately, I didn't trust him or the team, and my suspicions were proven correct a week later when I was made expendable in the NBA's expansion draft. The year before in 1987, the NBA announced that the league was going to expand to two new cities in 1988 and then to two more in 1989. In total, the league would be welcoming in four new franchises over the course of the next two seasons. First in line to get NBA franchises were the cities of Charlotte and Miami. The next year it was Orlando and Minneapolis. A week after Unseld told me that I'd be the incumbent starting guard, he called to tell me the Bullets would not be protecting me in that upcoming expansion draft. As part of the deal for the new cities entering the league, the new franchises were allowed to draft players from the league's current team rosters. Each established NBA team was only allowed to protect a certain portion of its players, leaving the remaining ones available to be selected in the expansion draft. Just a year after selecting me 12th overall in the NBA draft, I was left available for the expansion one. It was quite a precipitous fall from grace in the Bullets' eyes.

When Wes called me to tell me the Bullets were leaving me unprotected, I actually thanked him. "What?" he replied, somewhat confused. "Thank you," I said and I hung up the phone.

Truly, Kim and I hated to be in Washington. It wasn't the city itself. It was the working environment with the Bullets. It was uncomfortable, and we wanted to get out as soon as possible. The only good that had come from that year in the District was that I'd proposed marriage to Kim midway through my rookie season. I'd said, "Let's do this right." And I got on one knee and gave her a diamond ring. She said yes! With marriage in our future, we wanted a fresh start. Most players want to stay where they are, but I wanted out on the next plane to Charlotte or Miami. I'd tried my hardest with the Bullets, but it never felt like the team cared about me as a player. Like the city's newspaper, the team saw me as an oddity. They never thought I could help when it mattered.

Before the expansion draft, I'd heard that Charlotte was most interested in selecting me. I prayed they would. My time in Washington had felt even worse than my freshman year at Wake Forest. Normally, I was a fun-loving, gregarious person, always joking with everybody. But in Washington, I was miserable. As fate would have it, I was given my second chance. When the expansion draft occurred on June 23, 1988, the Charlotte Hornets selected me in the third round. Don't get me wrong. I'm thankful for the opportunity with the Bullets. They took a chance on me, and that's where my career started. I got to play in front of my hometown fans. I got to meet and learn from King, the Malones, Bol, and many others. It was a blessing, it really was. But I was ready for Charlotte. When my agent told me the good news, I nearly jumped through the roof. I was headed back to North Carolina where I'd already made a home for myself and I was determined to make sure Washington regretted watching me go. If they didn't think I could play as a rookie, then they'd have another thought coming in my second year. I knew I could bring value to a team. I knew I would be a valuable starter.

When you're a professional athlete, you don't need extra motivation. But it can't hurt to get some either. With the Hornets I had a new home. But maybe the best part was that the team had also selected my good friend Dell Curry in the first round of the expansion draft. Curry, who had been drafted by the Utah Jazz two years prior and was later traded to the Cleveland Cavaliers before Charlotte got him, would join me now to play with the Hornets. With any hope, we'd be the team's backcourt of the future. Everything felt right about my transition to Charlotte. Even the team's colors were better! I loved our uniforms. I picked No. 1 to symbolize that this was going to be my first *real* year in the league. As soon as I got to Charlotte, I saw the team's colors everywhere: teal jackets, T-shirts, jerseys. Our uniforms were the only ones in the league with classy pinstripes. Everything about the feel was *fresh*. There was a great deal of hype surrounding the team. North Carolina was historically a college basketball hotbed.

Now, the Hornets were set to usher in the big boys. The past year had felt like a total loss. Starting with a new team and a new franchise felt like I'd gone through a car wash and come out new again. I was determined to give it everything I had and succeed. To get a head start, I moved to Charlotte ahead of Kim and Brittney to mentally prepare for the season. I found an apartment before training camp started. I wanted to be settled as soon as possible. When Kim and Brittney did move in three months later, Kim changed all the furniture but admitted I'd found a nice location. Happy wife, happy life, right? Charlotte felt like home, but to Kim it still felt foreign. She was used to cities where it's louder and more active. Her support system was in Baltimore, including her parents and my mom and sister, all of whom helped with the kids. As a new mother, Kim really bet on us to move to Charlotte, knowing there are no guarantees in the NBA. I was grateful for her. For me, less action meant greater focus on basketball. I didn't want distractions.

But it took Kim some time to adjust to Charlotte. We knew we would make it work, though. Nothing good is done easily. Eventually, one of the reasons Kim began to feel more comfortable was the presence of Dell and his wife, Sonya. Kim and Sonya became fast friends and our kids, who were around the same age, did, too. Kim's parents also visited regularly, and we tried to visit them in Baltimore as often as we could, especially so I could see my family and little Tyisha. We got a good routine down. Things were settling in. Today, Charlotte is a bustling metropolis. In fact, it's one of America's fastest growing cities and one of its busiest banking hubs. But back then it was like a small town. Now Charlotte is the 15th biggest city in the U.S. and growing. But in 1988, when I got there, it was a lot quieter. Back then, there was no football team, no Steve Smith, Cam Newton, or Super Bowl appearance. It was just us: the Hornets.

The area has changed a lot over the decades. Although Native Americans had once inhabited Charlotte, the city was later settled by Europeans around 1755. During the Revolutionary War, British general Charles Cornwallis and his forces occupied the city. But they were driven out by what the general later called "A hornet's nest of rebellion." Hence, that's why we were named the Charlotte Hornets. Charlotte is North Carolina's largest city. The state itself is the ninth most populated in the country. North Carolina became the 12th state in the union in 1789 and it abolished slavery in 1863 when then-president Abraham Lincoln delivered his Emancipation Proclamation. At the time there were more than 331,000 slaves in the state or about one-third of its total population. I showed up in North Carolina 125 years later in 1983 to play for Wake Forest University and then again just five years later in 1988 to play for the Hornets.

I truly love North Carolina. It's my home and always will be. So, I think it's important to celebrate the city's achievements while also staying informed of its history—both athletic and political. Thanks to expansion, the Hornets were now part of that history, too. In 1988 during the team's first amateur draft before the inaugural season, the Hornets selected an affable, deadeye shooting guard named Rex Chapman from the University of Kentucky. Not only could Chapman shoot the ball, but he also was a leaper, a great dunker. As a player, Chapman had a lot of potential, and he and I became fast friends. Heading into the team's first season, the coaches and front office wanted to field an experienced team. The team's officials wanted to be competitive as soon as possible. They didn't want to muddle around at the bottom for very long. As a result, the front office more than anything else sought veterans like my friend Earl "The Twirl" Cureton, guard Rickey Green, and forward Kelly Tripucka.

Tripucka had a reputation as a good player, but he was somewhat past his prime and carried a big contract. We hoped he'd have something to prove. Cureton had played on teams with Hakeem Olajuwon, Thomas, Erving, and Michael Jordan. He always used to say I was on par with them athletically. I don't know about that, but I loved having my friend on the team. Our head coach that first year was the old-school Dick Harter. Before the season Harter told me that the starting point guard spot was wide open. It was going to be a competition between me and the team's other guards Green and Michael Holton. I was ready for a competition, but I hoped I wouldn't get jerked around like I had been with the Bullets. I wanted an honest tryout and for the best of us to lead the Hornets. That's the essence of basketball: skill should always win out no matter what. I went into camp believing what Coach Harter had told me. If he said it was wide open, then it was wide open. I knew the spot could be mine by the time camp was all said and done. I'd work every day for the chance.

As camp started, I'd never felt more prepared to be in the league. I'd played in a few summer leagues in Baltimore before moving to Charlotte to keep my game sharp. By now, I had a year's experience with the league and I saw how things worked. I'd seen what it took to make the playoffs and I'd seen how bad decisions could affect progress. There was a lot to manage in the NBA both in the game and behind the scenes. Travel and practice schedules sometimes changed week to week. But I was capable and getting even more comfortable. On the court, I was poised to score more. I wanted to see the game from a more aggressive perspective. But even more than that, I wanted help us win by putting my teammates in good position. The Hornets needed a leader. No matter how many veterans were on the roster, the whole experience was brand new for all of us. We needed a steady hand at the wheel, and that could be me.

I'd prepared and practiced my whole life for the opportunity to lead a team in the league. From dribbling up and down the steps in the Lafayette projects to running around in a hot Baltimore gym with bricks in my hands at Dunbar High. From surviving gunshot wounds to Wake Forest's bogus allegations. From the Bullets' inability to see me for who I am to *The Washington Post* calling me a freak. From coach after coach who constantly overlooked me, unable to see my skill beyond my height. Sometimes when I think about it, I grin at the miracle of it all. When you're going through hardship, you don't always know how you'll feel or what type of person you'll be when you make it to the other side. But with each day I felt more assured. I had Kim and Brittney at my side. I had a fresh start in Charlotte and I wasn't going to let this slip away.

MEMORY LANE
Rex Chapman

"Back in the day, they used to tell you your matchup for the night before the game. For example, if we're playing the Lakers, I'll guard Magic Johnson. The coaches will say, 'Rex, tell me about Magic.' And I'd say, 'He's big, he can post up, he can pass.' That sort of thing. Then they'd come to Muggs, and every night—it didn't fucking matter who we were playing—he'd say, 'Good defender, runs, can post up. And he's got a high dribble.'

"Me and Dell would sit there and wait for it each night! 'He's got a high dribble!' We were like, 'Well, yeah! To you, everyone's got a fucking high dribble!' But he was serious about it. Dell and I would sit there, kneeing each other, like *here it comes, here it comes!*

"But make no mistake, Muggsy belongs in the Hall of Fame. He was unlike anything I'd ever seen in my life. I had the good fortune of playing with great point guards in my career. In the pros I played with Scott Skiles, Muggsy Bogues, Kevin Johnson, Jason Kidd, and Steve Nash. There's only one player who reminds me of Muggs, and it's Jason Kidd. With my dying breath, I'll say that. Muggs could dominate a game. He would get mad if we would come down to double his man. If Mark Jackson or Gary Payton or Magic Johnson was down there on him in the post, it's just our defender's instinct to go help out. But then on the way down, Muggsy would say to us, 'Get the fuck out of here!' He didn't want the help.

"You can compare smaller players like Earl Boykins and Spud Webb and Michael Adams. They were all small scorers. But not a single one of them was a point guard. Muggsy isn't 5'7" or 5'5"—he's 5'3"—and he could run your team. He could pick up an opponent end-to-end, disrupt the opposing team's offense. He toyed with good players. Coaches used to say, 'Look, if you're dribbling the ball and you don't see Muggsy, pick that motherfucker up, or he's about to get it!'"

CREATING
A CULTURE

OUR FIRST HOME GAME OF THE INAUGURAL SEASON IN CHARLOTTE WAS a literal black-tie event. Tuxedos and all. Nearly 24,000 fans filed into the Charlotte Coliseum on November 4, 1988, dressed in their finest. They were so excited to have NBA franchise that people in the crowd wore full tuxedos and gowns. We packed the arena that day and, well, for years and years to come. There was a buzz in the city for the team—if you'll forgive the pun. That night ownership hired a symphony to play for the fans before the game. They pulled out all the stops. They wanted us to be good so badly. But in the NBA, you learn early on that you can't rush things. Even if you get lucky with a young All-Star player in the draft, seasoning and experience are much needed. No one walks into the NBA as an immediate MVP—not even Michael Jordan or LeBron James. As much as we wanted to win, we still needed to take our lumps.

In that first game, we came out raring to go—ready to represent the city and the warm welcome. We were slated to play the Cleveland Cavaliers, a solid team with a great starting lineup that included the talented center, Brad Daugherty; the lean scorer and defender, Ron Harper; the big forward, Larry Nance; and the sharp-shooting guard, Mark Price, who I knew from our days in the ACC. Our nerves were at an all-time high. The future hall of famer, Lenny Wilkens, coached the Cavs. And their team had hunger, skill, and experience. As you might expect, we lost the contest. But we did so by a whopping *40 points!* I shake my head thinking about it now. We were *bad* in that one. Yet, after the buzzer, the fans, almost all of whom had stayed to the end of the big loss, gave us a standing ovation. In that moment we knew there was nowhere to go but up, and our fans would stay with us the whole way.

To be appreciated is a terrific thing. That first season, the local Charlotte media dubbed our home gym, "The Hive." There was exuberant joy in the air. People cared. It was like everyone in the city had a new favorite thing to talk about. There was a new hope for the team's success. We were in the beginning of the honeymoon phase. But our team's first real highlight came that season when Jordan and the Chicago Bulls came to The Hive a few weeks into the year. It was Jordan's first time back to the state of North Carolina to play basketball since his days at UNC. That day, though, we got the best of him. We played the Bulls tight the whole game. Then on a last-second buzzer-beater by our lanky power forward, Kurt Rambis, we won the game. Rambis was known for his years with the Los Angeles Lakers and Magic Johnson in the '80s. I bet Jordan hated seeing him get that final bucket.

But that's sports. A game can change quickly and because of a fingernail. We all knew that well. We were a team of players nobody wanted, the island of misfit Hornets. While we were a lively bunch, I wasn't having the best time that first year. I wasn't playing very much—or at least as much as I'd wanted. Coach Harter, like others before him, still couldn't see past my size. He was disrespectful about it in fact. Harter would make fun of me to the media and in front of the team. One time he got on his knees in front of some reporters and said, "Hey, I'm Muggsy! Look at me trying to defend Patrick Ewing!" Then he got up on a chair and said, "Try to defend this when you're a midget like Muggsy!"

It made no sense. I was playing great in practice, and he saw that every day. As it happened, the owner of the Hornets, Mr. George Shinn, was all of 5'5" and didn't much appreciate Harter's insults. Shinn believed in me. But despite the owner's encouragement, I began to feel more and more discouraged by my lack of playing time at the hands of Coach Harter. In that season the journeyman guard Michael Holton was playing ahead of me, even though I beat him out in practice every day. But just as the season was starting to feel like Washington all over again, something changed. The fans began to cheer for me when I got in the game—loudly. Heck, they cheered for me *to* get in the game. They fell in love with what I could do and wanted to see more. When I got in, I didn't let them down, which only made them applaud more. I was becoming a hometown hero, which gave me hope that I'd have a real career here. I wanted to play well for Charlotte. Even more than the Hornets organization, doing it for the city and our fans felt paramount. They bought the tickets, they clapped in the stands.

During those first few years, the fans showed us so much love. In truth, a Hornets player couldn't pay for a meal in town if we wanted to. So, I wanted to succeed for them. On the court, I worked at it every day. Off the court, when I wasn't home with Kim and Brittney, I spent time with my teammates, Dell Curry and Rex Chapman. We all actually lived within five doors of one another. We were young and liked to joke and goof around with one another. In fact, our teammates started to call us the "Strawberry Hill Gang," which was the name of the apartment complex where we lived. Curry and I helped move Chapman in when he came to the team, and Curry at the time had a broken wrist, which just shows how much he liked his teammate. On game days, you could also find us in the back of the team bus, shootin' the breeze on basketball and everything else. Chapman and I talked about the season, how it was tough for both of us. He'd expected a bit of an easier transition to the league and wasn't performing like he or the Hornets hoped.

Most of us on the team were in long-term relationships and had families by now. But Chapman was a single guy, so he leaned on us for help. We were all so close that Sonya and Kim helped with his laundry. In return, we got him to babysit. Chapman's rookie season was bumpy, which was a feeling I knew a lot about. I tried to help Chapman like Moses Malone and Manute Bol had helped me, but he continued to feel frustrated. It can be hard for young players when they don't know where exactly they fit in on a team. It's made worse when the team is losing. Like me, Chapman knew how to fight. We worked every day at it. I'd always had to scrap and scrape to prove myself. Growing up shorter than all of the kids, I was doubted all the time. But that just made me more fearless. What did I have to lose?

I studied my opponents and I knew I could take control of a game on defense just by figuring out ways to pressure them. No one wants anyone inside their jersey. So, I was relentless. On top of that, I knew I could lead a team on offense with my speed, instinct, and vision. I was quick and I could read a defense like a *Sports Illustrated*. Other players couldn't touch me when I turned on the jets. I wriggled into the lane and scooped in layups. I couldn't dunk an NBA ball, but if I got a head of steam I could fly through the air. While we were fueled by the city's exuberance in that first year, we struggled both on and off the court. Our chemistry wasn't great, and losing, of course, didn't help. But I kept my head in the game and worked hard to get us better. If nothing else, we could build for next season. I wasn't going to let this team lag even if we weren't collectively the most talented bunch.

By the season's end, we'd finished 20–62. It wasn't awful for an expansion year, to be honest. We could have played worse, dispirited. On a personal note, I'd started 21 of the 79 games, in which I appeared, averaging 22.2 minutes. I'd led the team with 620 assists (7.8 per game) and 111 steals (1.4 per game) and likely total mph running down the court. The positive side of the season was that our team had led the league in total attendance despite our rather low win total. Our fans were behind us 100 percent, which was incredible. Even some big winners can't always say that. Our goal was to make the playoffs sooner than later. As an organization, we hoped to do so within our first five seasons. I was confident that we could and I knew that if we did I would be an important reason why. I thought about that constantly. While I didn't have the *greatest* sophomore year in the NBA, I was thankful to be on a team that had direction.

I was equally thankful for expansion. There was still a lot of work to do, but I knew we could do it. In the 1989 NBA Draft over the summer, the team made its second ever amateur draft selection, selecting bruising power forward J.R. Reid with the fifth pick. He was a local guy from the University of North Carolina and the kind of inside presence we needed. He brought toughness to the lineup. Truly, Reid was a good player, but unfortunately his addition alone couldn't fix an expansion team in its second year that struggled. Our sophomore season was just about as rough as our freshman year. To begin the campaign, we lost our first five games before getting a win against the newest expansion team, the Orlando Magic. After the first 21 games, we'd fallen to an abysmal 3–18. Our lineup fluctuated throughout. The locker room mood felt dark. I did my best to keep things light, but I wasn't feeling especially peaches and cream.

To me, the biggest problem was Coach Harter. Not only did he play slow, which didn't suit me or our team's skillset, but he also was overly disrespectful to the players, degrading people like Kelly Tripucka, me, Curry, and Chapman in the locker room and disparaging all of us to the press. During one halftime in our first year, Coach Harter came into the locker room and went in on each and every one of us. We were playing the Los Angeles Lakers and were down by about 22. He told me that "assists don't mean shit in this league, son." He told Curry, "You've been on three teams in three years. No one wants you!" He told the whole team we were a bunch of cast-offs. That was the last straw for me. If he didn't believe in setting up a teammate for a bucket, he didn't believe in the game of basketball as far as I was concerned. Even though I'd earned the starting point guard spot on the team, Coach Harter wasn't trying to make me better as a player or as a person. In fact, it felt like he wanted me to fail so he could bench me permanently. But I wasn't going to let him have that satisfaction.

Shinn brought Reid, Chapman, Curry, and I into his office to ask if a change at coach needed to happen. It seemed to me that Shinn knew the team needed a change, but he wanted to see if we agreed. I knew I did and I told him so directly. Coach Harter had to go. Soon after, Shinn fired him, and the team's assistant coach Gene Littles took over in the lead role. Coach Littles wanted us to run, which suited me just fine. When he took over, we got better. Although we didn't show it immediately in the record books—we went 2–20 in his first 22 games—everyone internally knew we were improving game by game and quarter by quarter. Coach Littles was much more of a positive person than Harter had been, and we all responded to that. It was a breath of fresh air. We finished our second season 19–63. However, it felt as if, despite winning one fewer game than the year before, that we'd taken a step forward in the eyes of the league.

We'd shown flashes of our real potential, and that was something to build on. We were no longer simply starting from scratch. In terms of my game, I'd upped my scoring average that year to 9.4 per contest. I'd started 65 of 81 games, averaging 33.9 minutes. I was one of the league leaders in assists (10.7 per game) and steals (two per game). I'd also won the respect of my teammates, who voted me the team's MVP that year. I could feel the future beginning to brighten, the clouds parting. But there was much more change ahead. Going into our third season, the team hired a new general manager, Allan Bristow, which I backed. I liked the move quite a bit. Bristow would be a good thing for my game. In the NBA at that time, the game was beginning to slow down thanks to physical teams like the New York Knicks and Detroit Pistons. As a result, there was a premium on post play and interior defense. Nevertheless, Bristow wanted to play with speed, and I dug that. Just because other teams wanted to slow it down didn't mean we had to, right? "I love guys who can press," Bristow said while praising me to reporters.

He told me he'd actually wanted to draft me in 1987 while he was working with the Denver Nuggets. Later, when I was with the Washington Bullets, he said he'd tried to trade for me when they weren't giving me minutes. Bristow had previously played and worked under Denver's up-tempo coach, Doug Moe, who loved to run and score. His Denver teams were some of the fastest and highest scoring in league history. I pictured myself on some of those teams and wondered just how many assists I could have racked up. I would have loved to play for Moe. Now, with Bristow behind me, I felt more confident heading into the new season.

With their 1990 draft pick that summer, the Hornets selected the talented wing player, Kendall Gill, a lanky, 6'5" guard from the University of Illinois. Although Gill was a great player, his selection immediately created a logjam in the backcourt. It was unclear how he, Chapman, Curry, and I would all fit together. At first, the Hornets thought Gill could play small forward, but he was better suited at shooting guard, which is what Curry and Chapman both played. Curry was comfortable coming off the bench as our deadeye-shooting sixth man, which unfortunately left Chapman the odd man out of the team's rotation, and he continued to struggle. I hated to see that. I didn't want him to be traded. But it seemed more and more inevitable. Chapman was one of my closest friends on the team and in life. The Hornets had high hopes for Chapman's game and so did he.

At his core, Chapman was a slasher, a tough player. He once scored nearly 40 points against Michael Jordan. He was someone who could hit a game-winning three for us in the playoffs. Although Chapman eventually did develop into that type of player—he hit one of the most famous game-winners in NBA history playing for the Phoenix Suns—he didn't do it for Charlotte sadly. That's one of the toughest parts of the league, seeing someone who you like go through a rough time, especially if you've been there before and know what it feels like. I knew he would bounce back. Chapman has a great spirit. Today he's an Internet star on Twitter, which is is great to see. He was fun to play with. I remember one game in Washington during our losing days in Charlotte he told a notorious D.C. heckler that our assistant coach was wearing a toupee. Our poor coach didn't hear the end of it for four quarters. One of the few highlights of the 1990–91 season in Charlotte was that the NBA held the annual All-Star Game in the city that year. The game down to a last-second shot by Kevin Johnson, and the East team beat the West.

The marriage between Charlotte and the NBA was going strong and here to stay. By our third year, my reputation as a player had grown, too. I'd become popular in both the city and around the league. I heard from more people how they appreciated my story because they were my height. I made them feel as if they could achieve more than what others thought. I really appreciated that. By our third year in Charlotte, I was one of only a handful of players left from the original Hornets roster, and one of those guys, Dave Hoppen, would soon be traded, leaving just me, Chapman, Curry, and Tripucka. In a way, the team was still looking for its identity. Our backcourt was solid, but our frontcourt was more limited. Reid wasn't having the early career success that everyone hoped. He wasn't dominating down low. Maybe it was the pressure of being picked fifth to play in his home state, but he couldn't make the mark we all wanted.

As a team, we could score pretty well. I was always looking for my team-mates. I had a clock in my head and knew to get the ball out before the alarm rang. But the problem was that we had little to no defensive presence in the paint. That's crucial for the NBA game, especially back then. We started our third season decently despite that. In November we went 8–7, the franchise's best mark for a month. But in December it fell apart. We lost 11 games in a row. We were playing fast, but we just weren't good enough, especially on defense. Coach Littles, true to his word, had sped up the team's tempo, but when you play with speed, the skill players need to play precisely, and the defense has to be steady. As a unit we just weren't up to snuff. We finished our third year 26–56. Better than the year before but still not playoff material. Gill was a bright spot, averaging 11 points per game. Reid did okay, too, averaging 11.3 points and 6.3 rebounds per as our starting center. We knew we were inching closer.

Thankfully, our fans continued their support. For the season our attendance nearly hit one million tickets sold for 41 games. My game, though, took a bit of a step back. I was putting in my usual full effort, but the coaching staff was trying different roster combinations to see what worked best. I was in and out of the starting lineup, which made it more difficult to find my rhythm. I started 46 games, playing 28.4 minutes. I averaged seven points per game and was again among the league leaders in assists (8.3) and steals (1.7) per game. I could feel that next year was our year and mine too. I believed we would all take a leap forward. Off the court, Kim and I finally got married. We had a great wedding, too, in the summer of '89. There were 200 people, including a lot of my teammates. A lot of the players shed tears. Kim and I also bought a home in the suburbs of Charlotte. Tyisha came to live with us. Kim and I were glad for it. Tyisha had been having trouble in school in the city, so we thought that her staying with us would be a good fit.

I'm an over-protective parent, so I was happy to have her with us. It was a good idea, too. As soon as she came to live with us, we saw a difference in her personality immediately. Tyisha could relax and focus on what she needed to in our home. It felt great to provide that for her. From age seven to 10 before she got homesick for the bigger city again and moved back to Baltimore with her grandmother, she ended up staying with us for four years. Not long after Tyisha had moved in, we found out Kim was pregnant for a second time. We found out the good news on Kim's birthday, which made it that much better. I was not-so secretly hoping for a boy this time. We'd had some issues trying to get pregnant again as a couple. So, when we found out Kim was expecting, we were very grateful. Kim is a great mother, and I tried to do everything I could for her when she was pregnant despite the rigors of the season. Then, in the blink of an eye on March 29, Kim went into labor with our second child.

Again, she went to the hospital on a game day. I was so nervous that I didn't know what to do. But our doctor practically shoved me out of the room and told me to leave the hospital to go play at The Hive, which I gladly did. I'm no good in hospital rooms. I thought about Kim the whole time. After the game Curry and his wife, Sonya, joined me back at the hospital. Our two families were so close. Sonya and Kim are like sisters now. They'd spend time together when Dell and I were on short road trips or they'd come visit us if we were on a long one. Eventually that night, though, it got so late that Dell and Sonya went home before we could welcome in the new baby. But at 4:52 AM on March 30, 1991, our son, Ty Jr., was born. I was thrilled! I imagined all the ups and downs ahead of us and just smiled. It can be hard as a parent in the NBA. You're away from home so often.

Brittney used to ask if I left so often because she wasn't important enough. Imagine hearing that as a parent! That broke my heart. But the NBA is a job, and I had to go to earn a living for my family. When the 1990–91 season concluded, Coach Littles stepped down as coach and took a front office position as vice president of the team. In his place Bristow came down from the front office to coach the team. Though I appreciated Coach Littles, I loved the switch. Bristow believed in me more than anyone but Shinn in the organization, and I knew I would thrive under his leadership. Bristow appreciated small guards. He knew we could play with the bigger guys. He told me he planned to run an offense dependent on passing. He said I was the perfect guy for the system, the perfect player to lead the Hornets. For the first time since my senior year at Wake Forest, I entered the new season as a team's starting point guard. I'd found my niche.

In the summer that year, Shinn arranged for me and Curry to play in a minor league baseball game. We played a couple of innings for the Gastonia Rangers of the South Atlantic League. I played second base, but Curry, who'd been drafted as a baseball player once upon a time, was the real deal. He got to pitch in the game. That was a fun day despite the game getting rained out. I even got to throw a base runner out. Finally, it felt like I had the right people behind me. The future was bright.

The cherry on the proverbial sundae came when the Hornets won the lottery to pick first in the upcoming 1991 draft. The big name that year was none other than the sensational Larry Johnson, the big, athletic player with the gold tooth from UNLV. Johnson, a Texas native, was a power forward who could jump out the gym and score with the very best. He was a true superstar in every sense of the word. There was no question about it; he was our guy with the No. 1 pick. Thankfully, the Hornets selected him first in the draft, and a couple days after that, I called Johnson to welcome him to the team. He was excited for the start of the season, and I told him, "Big Fella, if you work hard, I'll make sure to get you the Rookie of the Year."

He could tell I meant it. I could hear it in his deep voice with that heavy Texas drawl. But while winning the lottery was a high point for the team, it also meant that Reid would almost assuredly see a decrease in minutes. It also meant his days with the Hornets were all but numbered. The NBA is fickle. In one moment you can be the team's top draft choice and in another you might be looking at a trade and a new city. While fresh scenery can be welcomed, it can also feel like a hard landing spot after real rejection. I felt bad for Chapman and Reid because I also knew their plight. But in the NBA, you can't feel bad about much for too long. There is always another game, another chance to prove yourself. For me, that meant building chemistry with Johnson.

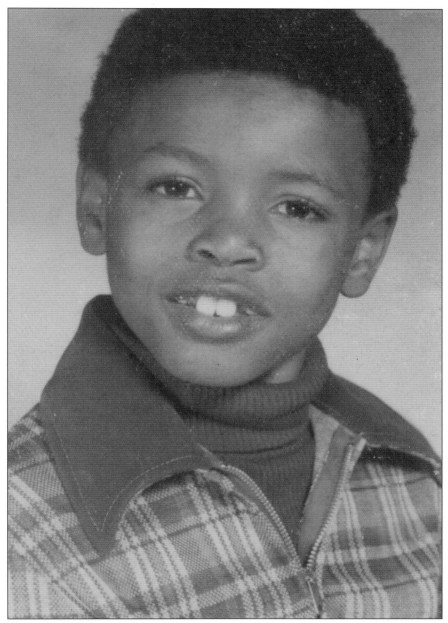

When I was just 10 years old. (Bogues family)

Kevin Bush, Eddie Bush, Gregory Harris, Dwayne Wood, Kimmie English, Stacey Fowlkes, and my brother Anthony visit for the 1991 All-Star Game in Charlotte.
(Bogues family)

My beautiful bride (Kim) and I exchange vows at our first wedding in Baltimore.
(Bogues family)

My late sister Sherron Bogues celebrates the special day with us. (Bogues family)

My daughters (Tyisha and Brittney) help Kim and me cut the wedding cake.
(Bogues family)

My date Tracy and I head to my senior prom at Dunbar High School.
(Bogues family)

While playing for Wake Forest, I dribble between John Salley (22) and Yvon Joseph (54) of Georgia Tech in 1983. (AP Images)

After the Washington Bullets drafted me in the first round, people always wanted to pair me with 7'7" Manute Bol in photos. I never liked that because it was only about our disparate heights, but I did enjoy spending time with Bol, who became a good friend. (Getty Images)

I defend Cleveland Cavaliers point guard Mark Price, who I also played against in college, in 1989. (AP Images)

I shoot over Patrick Ewing (33) and Charles Smith as we defeated the New York Knicks 110–103 in December of 1992. (AP Images)

My buddy, Larry Johnson hugs me during the final seconds of our 99–98 double overtime win against the Boston Celtics in 1993. The win was the first playoff victory ever for the Charlotte Hornets. (AP Images)

I high-five Alonzo Mourning, the No. 2 overall pick in the 1992 NBA Draft, who bonded instantly with me. (AP Images)

I set up to take a shot during the 1994–95 season. I averaged a career-high 11.1 points (along with 8.7 assists) that year. (AP Images)

I save a loose ball for the Golden State Warriors, the team I played for after 10 seasons in Charlotte, in 1997. (AP Images)

My buddy Dell Curry and I got to play together on the Toronto Raptors. (Bogues family)

I instruct Helen Darling during my stint coaching the Charlotte Sting from 2005 to 2006. (AP Images)

I horse around during a pool day at the house with Brittney (left) and Tyrone (right). (Bogues family)

My son, Tyrone Bogues, overlooks it all after Kim and I exchange vows and officially become reunited as husband and wife.

(Bogues family)

I blow out the candles at my 50th birthday celebration/surprise wedding while with family and friends.

(Bogues family)

MEMORY LANE
Larry Johnson

"When I was drafted, my agent and the people representing me were like, 'Muggsy's great! Muggsy is the best because he's a passing point guard. He looks for his teammates.' Coming into the league as the No. 1 pick, the greatest guard I could have had was Muggs. He was someone who looked out for the power forward. He wanted to make me better.

"Muggsy doesn't like when I tell this story, but this is what he said to me. It was midway during my first season, the 30th or 40th game. The Rookie of the Year Award was teetering between Dikembe Mutombo and me. And it was just me and Muggsy in the gym; we were the only two. Muggs, all of a sudden, went, 'You wanna win Rookie of the Year?' and I said, 'Yeah, motherfucker! I want to win Rookie of the Year!' All of a sudden, I went from scoring about 16 points per game to over 20."

TAKING FLIGHT

WHEN A TEAM ACQUIRES A PLAYER LIKE LARRY JOHNSON, THE FUTURE can seem almost blindingly bright. That's how it felt in many ways entering the 1991–92 season. North Carolina likes to dub itself as the state "First in Flight" because that's where the Wright brothers' first sustained flight took place. (The slogan is on many of the state license plates.) Well, with Johnson we were poised to hit the clouds! He was a once in a generation-type of talent. The word is "transcendent." There are a lot of players in the league who can score or rebound or defend. But few can do all three while also taking also over a game. Few can single-handedly will a team to wins. Few can elevate to that high of a level and do it in the playoffs, too. Those are the types of players we call "superstars." Johnson was a superstar. We knew it from Day One. Prior to picking L.J., the team debated between him or the 7'0" defensive-minded center, Dikembe Mutombo. Interior defense was often key to winning in those days, but superstardom edged that out ever so slightly. I hoped the team would get it right and pick Johnson. In the end they made the right choice.

L.J. was a talker, but he could back it up. And if anyone on the opposing team tried to rough me up, Johnson was there on the next play with elbows and something smart to say. He was one of the best trash talkers in the league. He had a great smile and arms the size of tree trunks. No one wanted to mess with him. Trash talk was a big thing in the league back then. There were some all-time great talkers in the NBA, including Gary Payton, Reggie Miller, Tim Hardaway, and Michael Jordan. Those guys never shut up! But good trash talk never crosses certain lines. Sometimes people think that because I'm short people were always talking trash to me.

But that actually wasn't the case. I earned the respect of my peers in the league. My game proved my height didn't matter. Even if someone did try to get personal, that never really bothered me anyway. I knew Johnson had my back and I'm from Baltimore. Trust me: I've heard worse. If anything, I'd have fun with it.

Johnson was a marketer's delight. He soon became famous in part because of his "Grandmama" character for his Converse shoe brand. To promote his deal with the company, Johnson put on a grandmother's dress, big grey wig, lacey Sunday hat, and ferociously slam-dunked on people in his commercials. It was one of the most successful campaigns of its time. Johnson (as Grandmama) even appeared on an episode of the popular television show *Family Matters*; he helped Steve Urkel win a two-on-two basketball tournament. With each game during his rookie year, he began to set the foundation for the success that would soon come for the Charlotte Hornets. In those days players stayed multiple years in college, so they were often ready to hit the ground running when they entered the league, especially if they were high selections.

L.J. had come out of UNLV after averaging a combined 21.6 points and 11.2 rebounds per game, winning the NCAA Championship in 1990 and returning to the Final Four in 1991. He was ready to contribute. He was an enforcer on the court. But off the court, he was gregarious and charming. Once I teased him for not knowing my name in camp. He thought my first name was Muggsy, and Johnson was shocked when I told him it was Tyrone. But we laughed about it. Our chemistry was infectious. It helped that he drew so much attention on the court when he had the ball. When he dished it, the other four players on the court had a lot of room to maneuver, more than we were used to. That is what superstars do: they make their teammates better. They bend the game toward their talents and abilities. I don't know how many open three-point shots Dell Curry got from a pass out from Johnson. The Big Fella and I had a connection, too. He must have had 100 alley-oop dunks off my assists that first season. I lost count.

We started slowly that season, but we knew we were gaining steam. To start the 1991–92 year, we went just 12–32 through January. But in

February we notched a 9–4 record and went 19–19 down the stretch. Johnson was unbelievable for us. He bounced off of people in the paint, and his first step was as fast as a guard's. He could shoot from distance and he drove defenses batty. There was one game against the Seattle SuperSonics in January that season when Johnson went off. It was just before we started to turn it around. We were up big in the game in the beginning. In the third quarter, we were up 75–58. But then the Sonics came back. They had their own talented players, including Shawn Kemp, who had 18 points and 12 rebounds in the game. But Johnson outdueled him, notching 24 points and 13 rebounds. In the fourth quarter, the game got close. With about 12 seconds left, Kemp gave his team a lead.

We came down the next possession, and Johnson couldn't finish a layup. But we had another shot at it after the ball went out of bounds. Down 116–115 with 0.7 seconds left, Kendall Gill got it into Johnson who shot right away. The ball rolled around the rim and dropped in. Johnson won it for us in that instant. That season we finished 31–51 for our best year yet. Teams couldn't take us for granted anymore. L.J. was too good, and the rest of us were complements to his big game. I ran point, and we had shooters and our star. If you blinked when I had the ball, you'd miss an alley-oop to Johnson or a pass for three to Curry. In his rookie year, Johnson averaged 19.2 points, 11.0 rebounds, and 3.6 assists per game and he easily won the Rookie of the Year, which I'd predicted on our first phone call. Gill had a breakout season that year, too. He averaged 20.5 points, 4.2 assists, and 5.1 rebounds per game for us. Those were excellent numbers for any starting shooting guard. Another of our wings, small forward Johnny Newman who was a good friend of mine, added 15.3 points per game for us.

I'd also had a good season, averaging 8.9 points, 9.1 assists, and 2.1 steals per game. I suited up in all 82 contests and started in 69, averaging 34 minutes. Already with a solid foundation, we were about to get our second star and make an even bigger leap. In the NBA draft lottery after the season, the Ping-Pong balls went our way yet again. We lucked into the second overall pick, even though we were far from the second worst team in the league. We were ecstatic. We knew we'd get one of two great college big men, who were both already household names. The choice in the top two was between Shaquille O'Neal out of Louisiana State University or Alonzo Mourning out of Georgetown. They were both can't-miss prospects. The consensus among the media was that Shaq was the better player (he would go on to beat out Zo for Rookie of the Year that season). But my personal favorite was Mourning. Shaq had all the hype and he could be flashy on the court with his big smile, but Mourning was a tough-minded, no-nonsense, rugged player. He had a snarling nasty streak to his game. Give me that kind of guy in the middle every day of the week.

No disrespect toward Shaq who's always been a friend of mine, but Mourning was right for the Hornets. I was glad the team got him with the second pick. What really hurt was that the team decided to trade away Rex Chapman to the Washington Bullets. I hated seeing my friend go. The NBA is a tough business. Now, all of a sudden, only Curry and I were left from the original Hornets roster. I had become a veteran and a fan favorite, which I enjoyed every minute of. Charlotte was my home now. In fact, I did everything I could to ingratiate myself with the city. One of my favorite things to do was dress up as Santa Muggsy for Christmas and hand out gifts to the local school kids. It still warms my heart thinking of them. I love to see kids happy, especially at Christmas.

I also remember around that time that a local radio station played a gag on the city for April Fools' Day. As a prank they reported that the Hornets had traded me. Dumbfounded the team would ship me out, the city actually went nuts for a few hours. The Hornets got so many calls asking what they were doing that they made an official statement that they hadn't traded me. But I knew how the fans would react if I ever really was! That reminds me of the time I pranked Reid. I had a newscaster in Charlotte record a fake broadcast that said he was traded for Rick Mahorn, which we all laughed about later in the locker room. But not every interaction with the media and fans was so jovial. One time a family of three showed up on my porch in Charlotte. It was a man, woman, and a baby in a stroller. I had no idea how they got to my house and I actually bought them bus tickets to get home. Later, I found out my UPS driver told them my address. The fans were certainly passionate in Charlotte. They were hungry for a winner.

We were building momentum, heading into our fifth season. Though we'd missed the playoffs in Johnson's rookie season, I had a feeling that we wouldn't miss them in the next one. The 1992–93 campaign would be our fifth as a franchise, and it had been our goal from Day One to make the playoffs in that year. That objective was on everyone's mind. But there was a new spring in our step. We now had a 6'9" star power forward in L.J. and a 6'11" star center in Mourning to protect the middle. I raced up court, handling the ball. The quicker I got up, the more time our stars would have to operate. I'd whip a crisp entry pass to either of my big guys, and they almost always scored if they got down low. Occasionally, I'd shoot a jumper just to keep the defense honest. I was a solid shooter—I shot 47.2 percent from the field the year prior and 78.3 percent from the free-throw line—but I much preferred to help set up a teammate. As a group we were ready to compete with the tops of the league.

Even though so many of the original Hornets were gone, I was glad Curry was still with me. We needed him. He was a deadeye shooter. He'd played great through his first four years with the team. His first year with the Utah Jazz and second with the Cleveland Cavaliers had felt disappointing, but he was a necessary player for us now. Coming to Charlotte helped him like it had helped me. In his first four years with Charlotte, Curry averaged 13.6 points, 2.1 assists, and 2.7 rebounds per game in 23.2 minutes in 268 games. More importantly, though, Curry was one of the best long-distance shooters in the league. He could stretch the floor for us and give Johnson and Mourning more room to maneuver inside because Curry always had to be guarded from deep. In an era when solid three-point shooting wasn't nearly as prevalent as it is today, Curry shot 40 percent from behind the line in the 1991–92 season to rank ninth best in the league. For the next seven years of his career, Curry would continue to shoot better than 40 percent.

Curry was also nearly automatic from the free-throw line; he shot 83.6 percent that season. When I got the ball off the other team's miss, one of my favorite things to do was race up court and find Curry coming off a curl for three. *Splash*. Today, Curry is known as one of the legendary shooters in the league ever along with Miller, Ray Allen, Larry Bird, Klay Thompson, and Dell's two sons, Stephen and Seth. Those are the guys who you'd want to take a last second three-pointer if your mortgage depended on it. Curry was as dependable as it got.

To begin the year, it took Mourning four games to join us. His agent had worked on his deal through the preseason, and there were disputes going into the new year. In the end it required some of us on the team (including me) to restructure our contracts to facilitate his new one. I didn't mind. I took a few bucks less that year and in return got some extra years added to the end of my deal. That meant stability, which I wanted.

I remember the day he joined us. Despite how big he was, he looked shy when he got on the team plane. I told him he could take a seat next to me, and we began to talk. But once Mourning entered the lineup, we started to win. From poverty to foster care, Mourning had already overcome so much in his life to become an NBA professional. As a rookie he was ready to dominate. We were 2–2 when he joined us to start the new 1992–93 season, but I knew we were poised for big things. In our eighth game of the season, we played at home against the Golden State Warriors. Mourning had 34 points and 14 rebounds, showing both strength and finesse. Johnson added 24 points and 13 rebounds, and I notched four points to go along with 14 assists and six rebounds. It was a breakout game for our dynamic duo, and we won 117–110. Not only was it great to have Mourning on the team, but the Hornets also signed another player that put a smile on my face.

A few weeks into the season, the team signed my former Dunbar High teammate David Wingate. We'd had some injuries on the wing, and Gate would provide the type of all-around defense and professionalism that we needed. It was great to have my friend on the squad. Sometimes I did a double take seeing him in practice, flashing back to seeing him with bricks in our hands and Coach Wade blowing his shrill whistle. We were coming together as a group. Early that season Zo showed he wasn't shy at all. During one game Mourning got in a fistfight with dirty Detroit Pistons center Bill Laimbeer. I don't want to condone violence, but that on-court boxing match made us proud. Despite winning two rings with the Pistons earlier in his career, Laimbeer was a notorious jerk. There's no other way to say it. To see Zo stand up to him with a few blows gave the whole team confidence that we weren't going to ever back down from anyone.

By Christmas we were 14–11, and Mourning and Johnson were each averaging double-doubles of 20 points and 10 rebounds per game. I averaged a near double-double, notching about 10 points and nine assists with two steals. When I saw an opening in the lane, I'd slice in and find daylight for a layup amongst the trees. Or if there was no shot, I'd kick it out to Curry for a three-point attempt. But most of the time I'd just look for Johnson or Mourning down low. While we were a good squad, everyone measured themselves against the Chicago Bulls. Jordan, Scottie Pippen, Horace Grant, and company had won the championship the season prior and were looking to do it again. In our second regular-season matchup against the Bulls that season, we lost 125–110. But in our third game that year, we beat them 105–97. In that one Johnson had 18 points and 19 rebounds, I got 11 points and 12 assists, Mourning had 19 points and 14 rebounds, and Gill and Curry added 19 points each. Jordan scored 28, and Pippen had 21 points, but we held the rest of the team down to get the win.

By the All-Star break, we were 26–23. Johnson had officially made the All-Star team as the franchise's first ever selection. I'll always remember how good Johnson was that season. With every dunk on somebody, he always seemed to finish the slam staring into the crowd with his pinky out like he'd just picked up a teacup. It was his signature. In April we went 6–3, beating the Bulls one more time for good measure by the score 104–103 in the second to last game of the season. By the end of the season, we were 44–38, the fifth best record in the Eastern Conference. We'd also sold out every home game at The Hive, continuing an ever-growing streak of 194 sellouts in a row. We'd had a great year and—seemingly in the blink of an eye—we were in the NBA playoffs. We'd finally done it after five hard years of trying.

The Hornets had risen to the level that we'd always wanted. We'd done it for the fans who'd long supported us. But the prize for our hard work? The historic Boston Celtics and my old Dunbar teammate, Reggie Lewis, the team's captain.

Truck averaged 20.8 points per game for the second season in a row. He was the team's bright future beyond their famed Big Three of Bird, Kevin McHale, and Robert Parish. In fact, many considered Truck to be Jordan's top rival. Truck had grown into a scorer who could slash and defend with the best of them. He was an All-Star the year before. I wasn't looking forward to playing against him in the first round. Unfortunately, though, we never really got the chance. Within the first five minutes of the first playoff game, Lewis fell. He collapsed on the parquet floor of the Boston Garden, sending shockwaves around the league. What made it worse was that no one had touched him on the play. He just lurched forward and fell. It was a non-contact injury, a sign of something internal and seriously wrong. Truck stayed on the court, dazed, trying to figure out what had just happened. We all were. The score of the game was 16–16 when he went down, but that didn't matter compared to the unknown status of my good friend's health.

If Lewis had twisted an ankle or a knee in traffic, that would have been one thing. But he'd just collapsed. It reminded many of us of Hank Gathers, another great basketball player who'd also fallen in a game because of an undiagnosed heart ailment. I was gravely concerned for my friend. I wanted him to be okay. I had no idea what Truck was going through or that would be the last time I'd ever really see him. I figured he would sit out the game, and everyone would reevaluate. I tried to move on. We had a series to win. To win in the playoffs, you need an extra level of focus. The games move faster, and every possession counts. I'd experienced the play-offs once before with Washington in my rookie season, but I was hardly playing for the team at that point. I'd watched the playoffs on television every year since then.

Now it was our turn to make a mark on the game. That year we'd gone 1–3 against the Celtics during the regular season. Yet, we felt confident heading into the series. The Celtics, a perennial playoff team, had all the experience. But we had the hunger. In the first game, the Celtics won 112–101. Though they beat us, we felt okay moving forward. We'd been on the road and didn't play well and yet we'd kept it close. It was first-game nerves. The Celtics were playing for their forward, McHale, who had already said he was going to retire after the season. Bird had retired the year before. McHale was an all-time great. But by the time our series came around, he wasn't the legend he once was. We knew we could beat them. Johnson and Mourning were young and strong. Plus, the whole population of Charlotte was pulling for us. The city's streets were barren during our games against Boston because everyone was watching us instead. Though we lost the first game, we knew we could come back in the series. We knew we could make the right adjustments on defense.

To start the second game, our plan was to stop the Celtics' pick-and-roll with their crafty point guard Sherman Douglas. That was on me, and I was ready to pressure him and give Douglas fits. On defense I liked to get low and press, often even full court. From a low vantage point, I'd have many angles to attack their dribble. And if I poked the ball away, it was off to the races. In truth once we got over the jitters of the playoffs in Game One, the hardest part about that series was that we didn't know about Lewis' health. Rumors were swirling about a serious heart condition. I knew I had to pick my team up and I was vocal that night, cheering them on and getting everyone involved in the huddles. We beat Boston in the second game on their home court in double-overtime 99–98. There were 17 lead changes in that one. McHale scored 30 points, but L.J. and Zo were beasts. Johnson had 23 points and seven rebounds, and Mourning got 18 and 14. I had a good game with the ball, adding 13 point and eight assists. We pulled it out because of them.

That second game would turn out to be McHale's last in Boston. In Game Three in Charlotte, Curry took over in the first half, scoring 19 points before the break. Johnson picked up where Curry left off, scoring 29 points with 11 rebounds. We won easily 119–89. That put us up 2–1 in the best-of-five series. We didn't want the Celtics to get a chance to play us in Boston for Game Five. We had to finish it off at The Hive in Charlotte that next one. Deep into Game Four, we were ahead 88–70, but we let up. We let them back in the game by taking our foot of the gas. We should have figured that the vaunted Celtics—even down in the series—would come back and play with their famed pride. The Celtics came all the way back, overtaking us and getting a 103–102 lead. With 21.9 seconds left, we set up a play. Johnson got the ball at the top of the key and drove to the hoop. He narrowly missed a double-pump that would've been the game-winner.

But when the ball trickled out of bounds, it was still our possession. In the final 3.3 seconds, and the game on the line, Curry, who was in-bounding the ball from underneath the basket, saw Mourning at the free-throw line and tossed it to him. Mourning caught it. He took one dribble, stepped back, and shot it. *SWISH!* He fell to the ground just beyond the three-point line and put his arms up in the air in celebration. If there was any doubt that Mourning or the Hornets had arrived, there wasn't anymore. We'd won the game…and the series. Our home crowd went nuts. Everyone cheered. Our whole team went crazy. We piled onto Zo like kids. The cheerleaders and mascot jumped on top, the announcers yelled, "It's over!" Fans stormed the court. But the funny thing was there was still 0.4 seconds on the clock.

We had to clear the court and actually play one more defensive possession. Boston had a chance to win it on an ally-oop on the next play but, thankfully, the Celtics couldn't convert. The ball rolled off the rim, and we'd made it to the second round! That gave us a ton of confidence. We'd surpassed our season's goal and our five-year goal. We'd done it for Charlotte. We were in the playoffs for the first time and also now advancing for the franchise and for us as players for the first time. It was big moment. A lot of celebration took place in the locker room. But after that we moved on because we knew in the next couple days, we had to face the New York Knicks.

In the next round against the star-studded Knicks, we quickly took some lumps. Their coach, Pat Riley, had the most playoff wins in history at that point. We soon learned why. Almost immediately, we fell down in the series 0–2. We'd played pretty well in both those games despite heckles from Knicks superfan and movie director Spike Lee. But we'd just let the games slip away toward the end. We didn't know how to win consistently in the postseason yet. Johnson matched up against Charles Oakley, and Zo matched up against Patrick Ewing. I took Doc Rivers.

It was a chess match, but we were outmaneuvered. We pressured the Knicks and tried to run as much as possible. We felt that we could—or even *should*—have been up 2–0. But instead we were down 0–2. New York won the first game 111–95 and the second 105–101. Collectively, we played much better in Game Three. In fact, I had my best performance in that one, notching three steals and a basket late in the game to take the lead. We won Game Three in double overtime 110–106. It was an exhausting game. I finished with 16 points, eight assists, and five steals. But as I said, things in the NBA can turn quickly. Despite playing so well in Game Three, I made maybe the biggest mistake of my career in Game Four. In the game's final moments, I lost the ball as I came down the lane for the tying layup. We lost Game Five 105–101. With that we lost the best-of-seven series. The magical season was over. We went back to Charlotte to lick our collective wounds.

A few days later, though, the city threw the team a parade. Charlotte was so grateful we'd brought the city a taste of victory that some 25,000 fans showed up to cheer us. Some even came up to our floats to get autographs as we drove along by. But the good vibes wouldn't last long for me. After some of the highest professional moments of my life that summer, I experienced some of the lowest and most profoundly difficult personal times.

On July 29, 1993, Reggie Lewis died in a gym. I'd been traveling all day and I'd landed in Tennessee to speak at a kids' summer camp when I found out the news. This was before cell phones. That night I called Kim just to check in. I began to tell her about the flight and my day. But she immediately cut me off to ask, "Have you heard?" When she told me Truck was gone, I burst into tears.

When I hung up with her, I called Coach Wade and cried some more. "It's not true," I wept. The story was that one or two doctors had cleared

Truck to play, even though many more thought clearly that he shouldn't. Truck had ended up collapsing just shooting around in a gym. The more I learned about the situation, the more it seemed as if it was all terribly mishandled. I couldn't believe my good friend was gone. The following year, when we played the Celtics in the preseason, I realized again how much I missed him. It hadn't sunk in until I looked over to see Truck on the Celtics bench, but he wasn't there. I couldn't help but cry all over again. I started that preseason game with red eyes. But the difficulties didn't end there. Three days after Truck's funeral, both my father and Kim's uncle passed away on August 4, 1993. It felt like two more scraps of shrapnel flew into my heart.

After I'd helped my father get out of prison, he'd had a difficult time adjusting to the world and staying sober. Ultimately and unfortunately, he gave in to the streets. He began using drugs with my brother, Chuckie, who himself was in and out of jail. Our father was admitted to a hospital with pneumonia. His body was broken, and he soon died from complications from the illness. I'd tried to help, but I wasn't able to do enough, I guess. I still get tears in my eyes thinking about my father there in his hospital bed. At his funeral I stood at the podium and remembered him as best as I could. I said that he was far from a perfect person but that I loved him dearly nonetheless. He did the best he could for us. I told everyone that I was going to step up in his place. Now I would provide for the family. I would be the man the family needed. It was on me.

MEMORY LANE
Dell Curry

"Those were some of the best years of my life. Our families had started to grow, our kids were growing up together. We were winning games. We were going to the playoffs. We had toughed it out through the lean years, the tough years, and now we were starting to play well and win games. It just made it that much better. Muggsy and I spent a lot of time together. That's why he's still one of my best friends because we were able to get through those tough times and then turn the corner and have a lot of fun together.

"I remember one time when I hit a game-winner against Golden State where our coach drew up a play, and Muggsy kind of audibled the play as soon as we broke the huddle on the court. I totally agreed with him! He had the ball in his hands. Who was I to say no don't do that? So, Muggsy changed the play ever so slightly. Muggsy said, 'No, this is what we're going to do.' And it worked. I hit a three, and we won the game."

10
PICKING UP
THE PIECES

THERE'S AN OLD SAYING, "WHEN IT RAINS, IT POURS." WELL, IN CHARLOTTE during the 1993–94 season, we got drenched. Along with all of my difficult personal tragedies, the injury bug plagued our team that season. Although we'd hoped to build off of the year prior and our trip to the second round of the playoffs, we were hobbled during much of the new campaign. Over the summer Larry Johnson had signed a massive, $84 million contract. He actually called me up and left a voice message to brag about it, saying, "You can now call me Mr. $84 million, Muggsy!"

I was overjoyed for him, but I also knew that with a big contract like that came big expectations from the fans and front office. Unfortunately, though, at the outset of the season, Johnson began to experience the worst pains of his career. He had a slipped disc in his back, and during the year, the injury caused him to miss 31 games and to play hurt in all the others.

Alonzo Mourning was also hurt for much of that season with a torn muscle in his calf and a bad ankle sprain. Zo, though, still played at an amazing level. Although the Big Fella only missed 22 games, he was rarely ever 100 percent for any. That year, too, our top rookie, Scott Burrell, hurt his Achilles early in the year. He had to miss 31 games himself. No NBA team can survive when its best players and top rookie are in and out of games. Needless to say, we struggled in a time when we hoped to get better. However, even given all this, we weren't a bottom-dwelling team. In fact, we kicked off the season pretty well. I was healthy most of the year, and we added two new players to the team that contributed right away. To everyone's surprise, Kendall Gill had demanded a trade out of Charlotte in the offseason. Maybe he thought he couldn't succeed as the team's third or fourth scoring option with us. Anyway, the Hornets sent him to the Seattle SuperSonics, and in return we ultimately received veteran swingmen Hersey Hawkins and Eddie Johnson.

Both contributed right away, and during the first half of the year, when everyone was still feeling relatively healthy, our team played confidently. We had talent and a nice reputation. At first, we got off to an 8–5 start in November and stayed around .500—meaning, we won about as many games as we lost—until late January. I was a blur on the court, trying to get ahead of everyone to either lay the ball in the basket or find an open teammate. I'd be at some guys' waists for a split-second as I jetted by them for a layup. I was in tip-top shape. I had my pregame routine down pat to prepare for each game, too. I'd get to the arena at 5:30 PM for the 7:30 game. I'd go into the training room to get some treatments before going out to warm up on the court. For my pregame snack, I always had peanut M&M's ready. I liked the crunch and the little energy boost.

After I went out to shoot, I would come back to sign autographs for the kids standing near the court. I did that whether we were playing home or away. I liked the rhythm of my routine. NBA guys will tell you: repetition and reliability go a long way in this league. But as Johnson and Mourning began to miss more and more games in the second half of the year, the team suffered and stumbled. Between January 25 and March 5, we only won *one* game, beating the Houston Rockets 102–97 in the first game back after the All-Star break. Near the end of the season, when Johnson and Mourning returned finally, we started to win again, earning victories in 18 of our last 26 games. But, in the end, it wasn't enough, and we *barely* missed the play-offs, finishing at exactly .500 with a record of 41–41 on the year. When our big guys had been able to play, Johnson and Mourning did their best, and we were a squad to be reckoned with.

Johnson gritted through a lot of pain that season. In a way, that contract wasn't the big gift everyone always said it was for him. It was a mountain of expectations on his back. It's as if all 84 million of those dollars began to demand too much of him (or anyone). It started to weigh on him. Nevertheless, our Grandmama remained solid. Over the 51 games he played, L.J. averaged 34.5 minutes, 16.4 points, and 8.8 rebounds. Not bad but certainly not his standard. He missed the All-Star Game. That season, Mourning, who gutted through serious calf and ankle injuries, played in 60 games. He was named an All-Star, though he had to sit out the game because of injury. Zo averaged 33.6 minutes, 21.5 points, 10.2 rebounds, and 3.1 blocks. It was incredible what he was able to do given his physical limitations that season. Mourning was our anchor that season.

But what kept our team afloat that year was defense and our play on the perimeter. That season Dell Curry played in all 82 games and averaged 26.5 minutes, 16.3 points, and shot better than 40 percent from three-point land. He won the NBA's Sixth Man of the Year award that season. Hawkins also played all 82 and he averaged 32.3 minutes, 14.4 points, 4.6 rebounds, and 1.6 steals per game. Eddie Johnson added 11.5 points per game and averaged a Curry-like 39 percent from three. Personally, I had my best statistical year, which included my best statistical game as a pro, too. It came in a blowout win against the Los Angeles Lakers. In that one I scored 14 points and dished out a career-high 19 assists, finding guys in traffic for dunks and in stride for jumpers. Few players in the league have notched that number of assists in a game, and all of them are greats, including two of the league's best point guards of all time, John Stockton and Magic Johnson. I was at the peak of my game. I even made a few people stumble and fall with my quick crossover dribble.

In total that season, I played in 77 games, starting all of them. In 35.7 minutes per game, I averaged a double-double—10.8 points and 10.1 assists—to go along with 1.7 steals and 4.1 rebounds. I liked to rebound and did it better than people expected. It was fun to get up above people who'd forgotten I was there. But to average a double-double was a career achievement and something I'll always be proud of. That's no easy task in the league. It came from looking for my teammates but also ensuring my willingness to score. I'd had my best year, sometimes notching 10 assists by halftime, while still pressuring the other team's guards full court and adding my share of layups and jump shots. Although our goal that season was to make the playoffs and exceed what we'd done the year before, we couldn't do anything about the injuries. They were the crash after riding high on the wave. Yet, in some ways, it was tremendous just to play .500 given that our two stars were playing through such pain. The NBA is a tough league in which to win. Each season can feel grueling with the preseason, constant travel, 82 games, and the playoffs (if you're lucky). There's a reason they call what we play on the *hard* court. That wooden floor can hurt when you dive for a loose ball or when you land awkwardly after a leaping layup. That hard court can do damage to ankles, calves, knees, and backs. It's cut a lot of careers short. It makes a 12-year career into an eight-year one or a five-year stint into three.

There's a lot I'm thankful for in my career, but surviving the punishment of the 1993–94 season is high on that list. It gave me even more respect for people like Kareem Abdul-Jabbar and Michael Jordan, who played in a historic amount of regular-season and postseason games. But what I enjoyed most over the course of that year was the energy and support we got from our fans. Basketball is a game that leans on the fans. We need their reciprocal energy. If aliens had landed in Charlotte and seen the passion and pride our fans gave us on a nightly basis there, they'd probably have thought we'd won every NBA championship there was. We finished first in attendance again that season, totaling just under one million total tickets sold.

Coach Allan Bristow was great for us that year. He kept us ready and motivated each game, even though it was a roller coaster of a season. Bristow's positivity sparked us. David Wingate was still on the squad, too, which helped me during the long season to know there was someone I could always talk to, along with Curry. But even Gate played in just 50 games that season. He also suffered some injuries, averaging 20.1 minutes and 6.2 points per contest. Today the NBA is much better about preventing and taking care of injuries. There are more team doctors and people paid to pay attention to that. In 1993–94 there was still so much to learn about kinesiology and player therapy. A lot of injuries could have been prevented if we'd known then what sports medicine knows now about recovery. But that's life. You do the best with what you got. During the middle of our winter losing streak that season, I'd called a players-only meeting to clear the air. The locker-room chemistry hadn't been great as we started to lose.

I knew that with Zo and Johnson struggling to play I had to be the voice of leadership. I was the floor general and the team's longest veteran, along with Curry. I wanted to make sure we were all on the same page. I wanted to make sure we would continue to put in our best effort. There was a little shouting that day, I admit. But I was glad for everyone to blow off some steam. If we hadn't all talked and aired it out, we may not have won enough games to even salvage the season. In many ways, I'm as proud of that 41–41 record in 1993–94 as I am about some of our better years in Charlotte. I always try to keep a positive and optimistic outlook on the world. I think it's part of being a good leader, part of the job of being at the front of the line. Although we suffered a few losing streaks, including an eight-game one before the All-Star break, we never let go of the rope.

The following year was the team's seventh season since expansion, and with a strong 1994–95 campaign, we'd prove that two years ago wasn't an aberration. We wanted to be in the conversation of the league's best. When the Hornets first began in 1988, it was practically impossible to predict where life would take the franchise over the next seven years. But here we were. We'd started with a ramshackle roster and then we had a strong team hungry to compete and win at the highest level. Achieving team success in a given year is the goal, but sustaining it is the real dream. We wanted another special year. I was in my eighth year in the NBA. I was smack in the middle of my prime. I felt at my peak physically, and my mind was sharpened with experience. I was ready to go to battle this season with my guys.

In practice the team had started calling Mourning, Johnson, and me the "Three Amigos." We told each other were going to make the playoffs by any means necessary. Our fans deserved another winning season. Although the last two were filled with a lot of ups and downs, the coming year would be different. It would be our fans who would carry us home. They were supportive and 24,000 strong at each home game even against teams like the sorry Los Angeles Clippers. The fans had supported us through highs and lows since that first black-tie blowout. It was infectious. As the team had solidified itself as a '90s mainstay in popular culture, it was time to keep growing. In fact, along with our pride, our outsized standing in the

American zeitgeist helped to raise the expectations for our team. Even our mascot, Hugo Hornet, was famous. A lot of people don't know this, but Jim Henson's company, The Muppets Studio, made the first Hugo Hornet costume. Jim's daughter, Cheryl, actually designed it. Hugo was a cartoon bug who could get the fans going.

The only other mascot in the NBA that rivaled the athleticism and charisma of our Hugo was the Phoenix Suns' Gorilla. The two guys under the costumes were actually former roommates! Sometimes, Hugo would go into his telephone booth like Superman and come out as Super Hugo in spandex and sunglasses. Super Hugo would really get the crowd going by dunking like Dominique Wilkins or Jordan. He'd have the people from the front row to the top of the rafters screaming their heads off. Heading into the new year, we were as popular as ever. We led the league in attendance six of the past seven seasons. There were busses riding around Charlotte with me, Johnson, and Mourning painted on the side. Teal Hornets gear was in shop windows and on the backs of the people walking up and down the streets. A lot of people bought it nationally, too. We'd see our colors at road games. Kids really liked it. The whole atmosphere felt special heading into the season.

That bounce-back 1994–95 season, though, despite all our excitement, started slow. We lost our first three games of the year, opening with losses to the Chicago Bulls, Cleveland Cavaliers, and Orlando Magic. After that, though, we got it going and went 14–9, raising our record to 14–12. We were like a locomotive going full engines. I was the conductor, racing with the ball, and the rest of the guys flanked me, ready for any pass I might throw them. It all clicked, and we went on a tear, winning 17 of our next 22 before the All-Star break. Both Johnson and Mourning made the All-Star team that season and we were on pace for our best season in Hornets history.

In the offseason the team had signed longtime Boston Celtics big man Robert Parish. He was an iron man of a player. Parish played 21 seasons in the league before retiring and was an All-Star in nine of them. That year Parish played 81 games for us, starting in four. He averaged 16.7 minutes to go along with 4.8 points and 4.3 rebounds per game. But more than any single stat, Parish brought a sense of both calm and toughness to the locker room. We could look to Parish for steadiness if the season felt like it might be getting rocky, which at times it certainly did. He'd battled with Larry Bird and Kevin McHale on the Celtics, going against the Lakers for championships in the '80s. Those rivalries saved the league when it was hurting before Jordan. Parish had seen it all—from the difficulties with individual ego battles to the collective joy and Finals exuberance. Though he was an older player, he was still nimble and tall. I had a few wrap-around and alley-oops to Parish in our time together.

To go along with his wisdom in the frontcourt, L.J. and Zo had their normal standout years. Over the course of the season, Zo averaged 21.3 points, 9.9 rebounds, and 2.9 blocks in 77 games, and Johnson put in 18.8 points, 7.2 rebounds, and 4.6 assists. But our most deadly weapon that year might have been the three-point shot. Three of our guys were in the top 20 in percentage from long range that season: Hawkins shot 44 percent, Curry shot 42.7 percent, and Burrell shot 40.9 percent. It's hard to lose for long stretches with that kind of reliability from deep.

We were one of the first modern, great three-point shooting teams in the NBA. We rode it to success. After the All-Star break, we again came out slow and fell in our first two games to the New Jersey Nets and Rockets. But then we picked it back up and won 19 of our final 32 games, bringing our end record to 50–32. It was the team's best victory total in franchise history and our first 50-win season. I'd started every one of my 78 games played, averaging 33.7 minutes, 11.1 points (the highest of my career), 8.7 assists (good for fifth best in the NBA), and 1.3 steals. I was also fifth in the entire NBA in free-throw percentage at 88.9 percent. As a team we'd finished just two games behind Reggie Miller's Indiana Pacers for the Central Division title and three games ahead of the vaunted Chicago Bulls. That was a small victory. But now the playoffs were on our minds.

The Bulls were one of the most interesting teams in the league that year. The giant story that season had been Jordan's return to the NBA after nearly two years playing professional baseball. Jordan had needed to get away from basketball and clear his head after his father had been killed in a freak robbery. He'd spent 18 months in the Chicago White Sox minor league system, changing his body to play baseball. But he'd decided to return to the NBA a few weeks before the playoffs that season. The Rockets had won the championship the year prior in his absence, and Jordan wanted to reclaim his throne. He returned to the Bulls near the end of the regular season, rejoining Scottie Pippen and coach Phil Jackson. That was the best combination in basketball. And as (bad) luck would have it, we were set to play them in the first round.

Each player to ever play in the NBA has had at least one deficiency in his game. For Bird it was his speed and that he couldn't jump. Magic wasn't a great shooter. Wilt Chamberlain wasn't especially clutch. Bill Walton was injury prone. You go on down the list and see that no great player's game was without a hole—except Jordan. I wish I'd gotten a chance to play with him. He was the only player I'd ever seen who didn't have a weakness. That's why to me he's the best to ever do it. But going into a game against Jordan, you can't play scared. You have to make sure you're prepared because you know he will be. He's only human after all, right? The Bulls, of course, had won NBA championships in 1991, 1992, and 1993. But Houston had won it the year he was away, beating the New York Knicks. In the 1995 playoffs, we were the Eastern Conference's fourth seed and had home-court advantage in the first round against Jordan and the Bulls. It was rare to be favored over Jordan—ominous, too. One of his nicknames was "That Black Cat" because he never brought the other team good luck.

Pregame at The Hive was wild. It got so loud at tip-off that I could hardly hear anything. The first game was close, but it was one of those where Jordan wasn't going to let his team lose. We pushed and pushed and scored back and forth with the Bulls, but Jordan was borderline unstoppable. He scored 48 points, and we fell in the series 0–1, losing 108–100. The next game, though, we blew the Bulls out. Mourning hauled in 20 rebounds, and we won by 17 points. We suited up to play Game Three just two days later in Chicago. It was a quick turnaround. But as a group, we'd spent the two days prior hyping ourselves up. We were ready. We knew this was a pivotal game. In all likelihood whichever team won this one would take the series. The Bulls had taken Game One, which nullified our home-court advantage. We had to take that back in Chicago. But, as the saying goes: man plans, God laughs. They were on a mission.

The Bulls routed us in Game Three in Chicago on their home court. We lost 103–80. In the fourth game of the series, we played them tightly. It was a low-scoring affair, a slugfest, a rock fight with several lead changes. Wearing No. 45 on his jersey instead of his normal 23, Jordan hit a three-point shot to open the game. He closed the first quarter with a three at the buzzer, too. That night the Bulls' talented Croatian small forward Toni Kukoc had a big game, hitting more three-pointers than I'd like to remember. (He shot 4-of-6.) Jordan was a killer in the fourth quarter, even though he looked more tired than I'd ever seen him. He still wasn't totally acclimated to NBA conditioning, especially after a physical series. In the waning minutes of Game Four, Hawkins hit a contested layup in traffic to put us up 82–81, but Pippen answered with a basket at the foul line on the other end to put the Bulls up by a single point.

We had to rally. In the game's final possession, we had the ball with only five seconds left. We were down by one point. Johnson got the inbounds pass at the foul line with his back to the basket. He faked right, spun left, and shot the ball. It fell short of the hoop, but Hawkins caught it mid-air and with a few tenths of a second left tried to reverse it in for the victory. But Jordan, trailing Hawkins, got him on the arm, and the shot fell just short. Of course, there was no call by the refs! They're not going to call Jordan for a foul on the last second of any game. So, we lost in Chicago 85–84. We were *this close* to forcing a final Game Five back at home in Charlotte. That one will always feel like both a game and a series that got away. Jordan, in many ways, was just too spectacular.

L.J. and Zo both averaged more than 20 points per game each and combined for nearly 20 rebounds per game. We had balanced supporting cast scoring from me (8.5 points per game), Hawkins (11.3), and Curry (12.8). But, in the end, Jordan, Pippen, and Kukoc were too much for our defense to handle. Their wings were too athletic. We were built for strength but lacked superior mobility. It wasn't a glaring weakness, but in the end, it was our undoing. Despite just coming off the baseball diamond, Jordan averaged 32.3 points per game in the series. Kukoc and Pippen added a combined 33.3 points and 13.5 rebounds per game. In the next round, though, the Bulls fell to the Orlando Magic and Shaquille O'Neal and Penny Hardaway. Jordan didn't have his legs under him. Orlando would go on to lose to Houston in the Finals. The Rockets repeated, winning back-to-back championships. Their best player, Hakeem Olajuwon, was a legend.

After our loss to the Bulls, the offseason brought some big changes. Despite Johnson and Mourning both being named to the All-Star team, the two didn't always get along great together behind the scenes. Both wanted to be the top dog on the team and both deserved it. Johnson had been with us first and had changed the team, and Zo came in and gave us that final piece that let us dream big dreams. During the offseason I also heard some criticism about how I couldn't lead a team to playoff victories. I knew it was crap, and if we had gotten a win against the Bulls, no one would be saying it. In my three playoff appearances with Charlotte to date, I'd averaged 9.4 points, 7.3 assists, 3.2 rebounds, and 2.2 steals. Over the course of four regular seasons from the 1991–92 campaign through the 1994–95 season, I'd averaged 10.2 points, 9.1 assists, 1.8 steals, and 3.5 rebounds in 318 games and I'd started in 304 of them while playing 34.6 minutes per game. Anyone would be proud of those numbers.

I was also one of the best and most careful players with the ball in the league. I was confident in my game and knew I could lead the team back to playoff prominence the following year. But our hopes for getting back to the postseason took a big hit when Mourning left us to take his talents to South Beach with the Heat in Miami. Since then, he's always maintained that he never wanted to leave, but that's how it worked out between him and Hornets owner George Shinn. If it had been a marriage, the divorce would have been a result of irreconcilable differences. So, the Hornets traded Zo to the Heat to become the anchor of the famed Coach Pat Riley's new squad. Coach Riley had just left the Knicks that summer, where he'd landed after leaving glitzy Los Angeles, where he and Magic thrived on the

Showtime Lakers. Then South Florida was his home, and Mourning was his anchor superstar. In Los Angeles, Riley had Abdul-Jabbar. In New York he had Ewing. Then he had Mourning.

As a result, the "Three Amigos" were no more. In addition to Mourning's departure, the Hornets traded away our defensive stalwart veteran, Hawkins. Two of our team starters were gone. I wondered what would come next. The NBA is capricious. What you thought was permanent can turn into a whole new scene overnight. I knew that well by now. But with roster losses also came new roster reinforcements. In the trade with Mourning, the team got back some great players, including high-scoring wing Glen Rice and tough-minded center Matt Geiger. For Hawkins we got Gill back, which I was happy about. But we also had to ship out Gate, which I was sorry to see. We still had L.J. and the run-and-gun offense that Coach Bristow instituted. There was hope. We were ready for another strong year. The only problem was that I wouldn't be healthy for it.

MEMORY LANE
David Wingate

"It was unbelievable to play on Charlotte with Muggsy. That's when me and him really became close. He's like my brother. Growing up, him and Reggie Williams were closer than me and him at first. But once we hooked up in Charlotte and lived around the corner from each other, we became even closer. He used to always have people over at his house.

"I remember when Chris Paul was there. They'd all come to Muggsy's house in the summer time, and Muggsy would talk to them, show them things, teach them the game mentally. I've seen him do that for years and for a lot of players. The one thing I want people to know is just how good Muggsy's heart is. He wouldn't turn you down for nothing. Muggsy is one of the best guys I have ever met in my life. I'm so privileged to be a friend of his."

SPACE JAM

MICHAEL JORDAN DIDN'T WIN THE NBA CHAMPIONSHIP IN 1995. THE Houston Rockets did, going back-to-back after beating the Orlando Magic and then the New York Knicks the year before. But after the loss to end the season, Jordan rededicated himself to hoops and had two goals: to turn his baseball body back into a full-time NBA basketball body and to shoot a movie starring him and Bugs Bunny called *Space Jam*. To do both over the summer, Jordan had a gym built directly next to the *Space Jam* soundstage in Los Angeles. During the day he shot the movie for 10 hours and then he'd shoot hoops in pick-up games with the best NBA players at night for three or four more hours. It was an amazing feat that demonstrated Jordan's drive. He wanted to show he was still the king of the NBA. He wanted his crown back and he would do whatever it took to make sure he achieved that, starting that summer in L.A.

In the end Jordan proved prescient. He went on to win the next three NBA titles, and *Space Jam* was a big box-office hit. In the movie small, gun-wielding aliens came to Earth to steal Bugs Bunny, Porky Pig, and the whole Looney Tunes gang. The aliens wanted to take them back to their home planet to force them to work at an amusement park. But Bugs and co. convinced the aliens that they deserve a chance to defend themselves. Thinking the puny aliens were too small, Bugs challenged them to a game of basketball. But here's where the twist came in: the aliens have a trick. They traveled to NBA games and took the talent from five superstars: Charles Barkley, Patrick Ewing, Shawn Bradley, Larry Johnson, and me. (It helps to share an agent with these guys!) The aliens stored our talents in a glowing basketball and absorbed them to become giant, scary foes known as "The Monstars."

When the aliens took my powers in the movie, I spread out my arms like a bird and shook like a ghost was taking over my body. I grin watching it now. The Monstar who got my skills was, of course, the smallest one. His name was Nawt, and he was short and red and very hyperactive. But because Jordan was out playing baseball, he was safe from the Monstars. The aliens didn't snag his powers because he's on the golf course between batting practices. Facing The Monstars, Bugs and the Looney Tunes then recruited Michael off the golf course (interrupting his game against Larry Bird and Bill Murray). After a little convincing, Michael agreed to play against the aliens for the Toons' freedom. Biases aside, *Space Jam* is a great movie, especially for kids, and we had a blast making it. *Space Jam* also reminds me of one of my favorite movies I saw as a kid, *The Fish That Saved Pittsburgh*, which starred Julius Erving. There was a character in the movie named Tyrone, so that made me love it even more.

When I watch *Space Jam* today, I'm impressed by how good Jordan's performance is. In some ways, the movie was similar to *Who Framed Roger Rabbit*, which also involved a lot of cartoon animation and some real-life actors. Jordan had to act as if Bugs and the Tasmanian Devil were right there with him, but it was all a green screen. In the movie Jordan could have chosen anyone to be his co-stars, but that he chose me was a real honor. After having played against him ever since college, we were in the hit Warner Brothers movie together. The only problem was I'd recently injured my left knee and had to have arthroscopic surgery to repair it in August after the 1994–95 season. Although I'd gotten the role in *Space Jam* before that, my injury almost caused me to lose the role to my good friend, Tim Hardaway, the All-Star point guard of the Golden State Warriors. They actually brought him in to read my lines.

Thankfully, everything worked out in the end, and I kept my job. In fact, if you look real close, there are two scenes in the movie when I'm on a dolly they made to pull me around to make it look like I was walking. I moved my shoulders for added affect. The first scene came when all of the players were walking with a doctor through a hospital, talking about our problem. I'm there side-by-side with him, as the big guys behind us hit their heads on the doorframe. The other scene came when we were trying to find out what to do from a fortune-teller. When we got up from her table, I had to get pulled away. In a third scene, I got to lay on a psychiatrist's couch. I didn't have to walk for that one. The doctor wonders about my relationship with my mom, and I told him I loved my mama. It was fun to get to mention her in the movie. In the film's final scene with our powers back, I had to dribble the ball. But I just stood stationary, dribbled through my legs, and passed it off.

Later that summer, we were all cast in the popular music video for the famous rock band Hootie & the Blowfish. Zo and I actually have Grammy plaque our basement from being in the Hootie & the Blowfish video. Their platinum, chart-topping hit "Only Wanna Be With You" was all over the radio, and the band members chose to play us in a game. We won, of course! I had so much fun working with the guys and the band. L.J. hates it when I tell this story, but there was one morning when we were all shooting around in the gym, and he decided that he needed to get a haircut at that time except the only barber there had never cut Black hair before. So the guy actually gave Johnson a bowl cut, and we had to cancel the shoot that morning until he could find another barber to fix it. It was truly hilarious!

Another great memory from those shoots was watching the nightly pick-up games in the gym that the studio had built for Jordan. I couldn't play in the games because of my knee unfortunately. But there were so many greats in that makeshift gym—from Jordan to Reggie Miller, Patrick Ewing, Dennis Rodman, Juwan Howard, Chris Webber, and others like Pooh Richardson and Chris Mills. Jordan talked trash the whole time to all the guys. He wanted to get in their heads from the start. He was learning each player's game as he got into their psyches. It was masterful to watch. During the day as we shot *Space Jam*, we didn't know exactly what the final product would turn out to be. Sometimes it can be hard to see the forest for the trees. But the movie turned out to be a classic sports movie. It's made hundreds of millions of dollars, and the toys made even more. It's a family movie, so you know I love it.

Space Jam is especially fun for kids to watch. It's got a great plot, funny characters like Bugs and Porky Pig, and some of the best actors in the business like Murray and *Seinfeld*'s Wayne Knight. What more could you want? As a production we wanted to show kids they could do anything if they worked hard—even defeat evil cartoon aliens. *Space Jam* took about 10 months to shoot, but a lot of that was Jordan working against the green screen. He filmed some scenes in a full 360-degree green room with motion trackers while NBA players in green suits ran around and actors pretended to be the Looney Tunes characters. The whole production was massive and cutting edge. Once *Space Jam* came out, Siskel & Ebert actually each gave the movie a thumbs up, and one of the songs on the soundtrack won a Grammy Award.

After it was a big success, everyone wanted a sequel. At the time, I didn't think there should be one. It was great on it's own, and a lot of the times when studios make sequels, they come out pretty bad. But I'm glad now that LeBron James has made his own version now. He's carrying Jordan's torch as the face of the NBA and so he can carry the *Space Jam* torch, too, in my opinion. James has done a lot of good for the game on and off the court. He serves his community admirably—from social justice to financial investment. I'm proud to see what he's done in Hollywood and on the hardwood, too. Jordan carried the torch for a long time after Magic Johnson and Bird, Kareem Abdul-Jabbar, Dr. J, and Bill Russell carried it. Today James is a player, but he's also an ambassador, a modern-day statesman. Like Jordan, James embodies what *Space Jam* is all about. My favorite thing about *Space Jam* is its positive message.

In the end Jordan and the Looney Tunes come back from a major halftime deficit and are beginning to believe they can beat The Monstars. Jordan doubles down on his belief in his team so much so that he puts his own personal freedom on the line in exchange for the chance to get our powers back if the Toons win the game. Jordan bets on himself, believing in his ability and his team. Although I know it's only a fun movie, that's still an important message for kids to hear. You don't need to steal the talent of anyone else; you can get better on your own. Play your game, just be you. Accomplish your goals, the ones *you* want to work on. It takes perspiration as much as it takes inspiration. Those are the things I learned as a kid in Baltimore with Reggie Williams and my coaches, and it was great to see them on the big screen in *Space Jam*. The movie concludes with Jordan going back to Chicago and winning more championships with the Bulls. It was prophetic. Michael would go on to win again in '96, '97, and '98.

But while Jordan and James are well known for their big movie roles and plethora of commercials, I was doing all right for myself in that department in the mid-1990s, too. In fact, in 1993 Raycom Video released the popular VHS tape *Don't Tell Me No: The Muggsy Bogues Story*, which told fans about my life up to that point. A couple years later in 1995, I got my very own action figure. It was made by the Starting Lineup toy brand, and the pose had me dribbling the ball to start a fast break. I still have a few of those somewhere; maybe I'll give them to my grandkids one day. Around that time *Jet* magazine wrote a big story about my life as an underdog. I was also in some pretty big TV commercials. One was for Sprite, which told the story of "Muggsy versus Goliath." The tagline in that one was: *"Height is nothing. Thirst is everything."* I really liked that. The commercial was all over the TV, too. I went against a big player and ran circles around him and through his legs before dunking the basketball. The commercial had this big close-up of my smiling face that everyone in my family gave me a hard time about. My favorite part was after I'd dunked all my teammates put me on their shoulders, and I raised a victorious fist in the air.

There was another commercial that I did for AT&T. It was for "small businesses" and how they can do well even if they're not giant corporations. Around then I was a guest on David Letterman's late-night show and got a cameo on *Saturday Night Live* when Barkley hosted, and Nirvana was the musical guest. RuPaul was there that night, too. I really enjoyed that shoot. Barkley was doing a skit for the show, "Charles Barkley's Big, Tall & Black Men's Store." The idea was funny. But what do you do to make a skit like that better? Bring in Muggsy Bogues, of course! I came in through the dressing room with a big smile on my face wearing a suit that was, well, way too big. I thanked Barkley for the "free alterations," which I would most definitely need. Everyone got a good laugh from that one.

A few years later in 1996, I played a guest role on an episode of the NBC Saturday morning show *Hang Time*, which starred Anthony Anderson and my buddy and former NBA standout, Reggie Theus, as the coach. The episode was called, "Short Cuts," and it was about one of Theus' players, Vince, taking steroids to improve his game. Vince gets into a physical fight with his teammates. I come in to tell him he doesn't need drugs to get better. There are no short cuts to hard work. Look at me: I made it without drugs, and you can, too!

Although all of that was great, I have to admit one of my favorite things from that era was being in the *NBA Jam* video games. It had all the teams and the star players. For the Charlotte Hornets, which many said were the best team in the game, *NBA Jam* featured L.J., Alonzo Mourning, and me. I liked to play as myself, running up the court, dishing to Zo or L.J., shooting three-pointers (which I'd hardly ever do in a game), and even dunking! One of my favorite moves was to hit so many shots in a row that the game's audio would say, *"He's on fire!"* The ball would come out of my hand in flames, and it would be nothing but net, burning the twine.

There are cheat codes in the game to unlock famous celebrities like George Clinton. I wish they had a code for my old Dunbar team. That would have been great. But no matter how often I think of this stuff, I always remind myself to keep a level head and to stay grounded. Don't get too high with the highs or too low with the lows. Never believe you're more than you are and never forget where you come from. These days I also teach the game at a lot of camps and clinics. I do as many speaking engagements as I can. And a lot of the kids I talk to are shorter than me, but they likely won't be for long. Seeing me helps them to believe they can be in the NBA, too, or at least play college sports one day. It helps them to think they could be in movies like *Space Jam* or appear on television with Letterman or get their own commercials. Sometimes I can see their minds working as they stare at me talking about basketball. They're thinking, *He's my size! I can do it, too!*

That makes me more proud of what I've accomplished in my life. But I'm no fool. I know none of this would have happened if I wasn't a good basketball player who put up numbers and made my team better. If I was averaging one point and one assist in three minutes of garbage time on a team that never made the playoffs, no one would have called me on my phone or sent me any movie job offers. But it was because I'd worked each step of the way—from the Lafayette projects and the rec center, to city leagues, to Southern High, from Dunbar to Wake Forest, from FIBA to the USBL, from the Washington Bullets to the Hornets, from preseason to the playoffs. It was only then after starting on Charlotte and playing in the postseason twice and averaging a double-double that Jordan and *Space Jam* called. It was only then Letterman and *Hang Time* and those other commercial jobs looked for me.

I knew I could control the amount of time I put into my game; that was maybe the only thing I could ever control. I told myself I would always do the most I could and the best I could. I owed that to my family, my friends, and my fans. I owed it to those who looked up to me and to those who, like my mother, have helped put me in a position to achieve my dreams and succeed. I owed it to my daughters and to my son. I owed it to my wife, Kim. But I also owed it to myself. I fought back a lot of tears in those early years and a lot of jokes pointed at me during much of my career. Even today it comes up in every interview and every media appearance. If I'd let my height stop me, where would I be now? Nowhere.

One thing I've learned over the years is that no one else knows what's good for you better than you do. People can give you advice. They can offer you their own experience. But in the end, you're the one who has to make the choice for yourself. No one will live your life for you. I wanted to say I did all I could for my family and me. That's the mentality I had going into our next season in 1995–96. Yes, I had injured my left knee pretty bad and I was out for most of the year, but I could still do things to help the team win on a nightly basis. We'd lost Zo to the Miami Heat in a trade and I was out, too. L.J. was the lone amigo left, but I wasn't about to leave him hanging. We'd been through too much. We would get through this together, too.

MEMORY LANE
Brittney Bogues

"I remember going to games during the week and having to change our clothes to our pajamas in the car so we could go right to sleep as soon as we got home because we had school the next morning. I remember all the Hornets chants, the songs. I remember playing basketball with Stephen [Curry] in the arena and growing up in a town where everyone knew who your dad was. I remember it feeling like a family, like a big family. The NBA has changed a bit now, but back then, all the players' kids went to school together; half of the teammates lived in the same neighborhood. We all traveled together. Stephen was the only boy at all my birthday parties. He was my first boyfriend. He actually gave me my first diamond ring."

12
INJURY AND RECOVERY

IN OCTOBER JUST BEFORE THE START OF THE 1995–96 SEASON, I GOT A call from my mother. She was exhausted, at her wit's end, drained, and nearly shattered. She didn't know what to do with my oldest brother Chuckie. At 37 years old and seven years my senior, Chuckie was supposed to be past the partying lifestyle, past the self-destruction that comes with it, too. Instead, he was right in the middle of it. He was using cocaine as often as people smoked cigarettes. My mom asked if I could help. "If you don't take him and move him in with you," she told me, "he's going to die."

I always listen to my mother. So, Chuckie came to my house in Charlotte and moved in. He'd admitted, "I'm tired of doing what I've been doing to myself. I'm tired of doing drugs." I knew I had to help him. I threw out the liquor bottles. I put non-alcoholic beer in the fridge. I checked the guest room and made it safe for him to go through rehab right there—cold turkey. He didn't want to go to a rehab center for six months. To him, that felt like prison. So he came to stay with me.

I bought Chuckie a red bathrobe that I gave to him when he arrived. I did whatever I could to help him feel at home. At that time if you were to look at my life on paper, it had never been better. But behind the scenes it was coming apart. Not only was Chuckie battling what he was going through, but my marriage with Kim also was falling apart. I didn't talk about any of this with anyone on the Charlotte Hornets. I didn't want it to affect my game. But it was eating me up off the court. Kim and I weren't doing well. The life of a professional basketball player can be tough on a family, and I didn't make it a whole lot easier for her and the kids. I'd just signed a new contract and I wanted to be sure to dedicate everything I had to the Hornets, to earn every penny. But at times that was at the sacrifice of my family. I also admit to some unseemly behavior, too, which further put a wedge between us. Eventually, our relationship broke down, and she said she wanted to leave.

By 1995 Kim was a mother to three children, and I was often not home because of game obligations and road trips, practices, or the media appearances I did at the time. Kim's parents would come down to help, but that wasn't enough for her. To make matters worse—and I don't mean this the wrong way—but I had a lot of fans, and many of them were women. Kim called them my "groupies." It always bothered her when they would come up to me after games. She didn't mind fans coming to say hello (unless we were about to eat dinner). In fact, she said it was honorable to sign autographs and take pictures. But she hated all the female hangers-on that would inevitably pay me attention. Eventually, she couldn't help but think the worst. And she wasn't always wrong. Trust collapsed, and before the 1995–96 season. Kim left me, taking the kids.

We'd been married for seven years. But we'd grown apart unfortunately. Kim was tired of being "Muggsy's wife." She needed to find herself. Later, she would go back to school and eventually find a successful career working with HBO. But at the time, she just needed a place to start her own future. She took the kids to the Charlotte suburb of Huntersville. I still cared about her and I knew she still cared about me. Leaving hurt us both, but I didn't give her much of a choice after a while. Kim didn't marry me seven years before to stay home while I roamed the country. She married me because she wanted to make a life with me, but that life was eroding in front of us. We needed space. I'll always regret hurting her and by extension our family. I knew I'd do the best I could to be in my kids' lives, even though Kim and I had to split. I was alone now but not for long. That's when Chuckie came to the house and when we began an important journey together.

Throughout our lives, I'd always helped Chuckie with $20 here, $10 there, whatever small stuff he wanted. But now we both needed each other in a much bigger way. It was an important moment for us as brothers. I didn't want to lose him. I'd already lost so many. Sometimes when I came home during those first few weeks, I'd see him shaking underneath the bathrobe I'd given him, going through horrible withdrawals. Sometimes I could hear Chuckie moaning and screaming from across the house. But slowly we got through it. The first six months were the worst. Chuckie went through it all in the guest room above the garage. It was the same house I'd lived in throughout my entire time with Charlotte. It was in the suburbs, and to my family, that might as well have been Kansas. The closest grocery store was half an hour away by foot, and Chuckie wasn't driving anywhere. It was quiet where we lived—unless Chuckie was really hurting.

When he wasn't feeling well, he would shake. It brought tears to my eyes. He couldn't control it. He threw up in the living room. I'd clean it up. Sometimes Chuckie would scream, saying he was getting the demons out of his chest. I'd bring him dinner, and he couldn't eat it. I wondered if Chuckie staying with me was good for him. I wondered if doctors could help. But Chuckie wouldn't allow it, and I didn't want to abandon him there. Slowly, though, he began to improve right before my eyes. He stopped throwing up. He screamed less and then not at all. Then one day he stopped me, looked me in the eye, and said he wasn't going to mess up again. We'd gotten through the worst of the storm together. I hugged my brother for his hard work. I was proud of him. I knew it could easily have been me if a few things in life had gone the other way. I loved Chuckie and I was grateful we'd done it together.

Once Chuckie was past the worst of it, he started to stand out on the terrace that overlooked the backyard and watch me and my friends shoot hoops in the yard. I had a basketball court out back there painted in Hornets colors, of course, and I'd have friends, pros, and up-and-coming local kids stop by to shoot around and shoot the breeze. It was informal, but a lot of great players came by that back yard, including Steph Curry, Chris Paul, Alonzo Mourning, David Wingate, Dell Curry, and Larry Johnson. Chuckie would stand on the terrace smoking a cigarette and talk trash as we shot. I loved it. I loved seeing him happy. He'd shout while we played H-O-R-S-E. It was wild seeing someone like Dell Curry miss a free throw because Chuckie was hollering. Chuckie became a favorite of all the people that came to the house. To this day, he's always with me.

But though Chuckie was past the worst of his plight, I was still smack-dab in the middle of mine. Watching my marriage fail depressed me. When Kim and I were together, we had regularly attended the Central Church of God in south Charlotte. After she'd left, I went back there one Sunday to pray. On my knees, I told God, "All of this is more than I can handle."

Kim was right. I'd taken her for granted. I'd left her with the responsibility of keeping our home together. She had dreams of her own, and I hadn't considered them. Tunnel vision, I'd call it. It had taken so much to get from Baltimore to the NBA that I didn't think about much else. Kim began to see me as arrogant as a result. I'd let the glamour (and groupies) cloud my brain. Now I was praying and paying for it. Kim had grown tired of people just calling her "Muggsy Bogues' wife." She deserved much more.

Not long after, Kim took the kids to New York City, where she began to start her career. Ty Jr. was five, and Brittney was nine, and I promised them I would always stay in touch. Even though their mom and dad were no longer together, I would be the best father I could. I would always be a caring father. I wouldn't abandon them. That's not how I was raised. I would call them every day, and they could come visit anytime. Each time Tyisha visited for holidays or I talked to Ty and Brittney on the phone, I would always make sure to reinforce one thing: they can do whatever they want to in life. I always told them the words "I can't" aren't in your vocabulary. I'd learned that from Bob Wade. I made sure to talk to each of my kids every day—if not twice a day.

On top of all of this, I had to undergo rehab for my left knee after torn cartilage necessitated arthroscopic surgery. I was supposed to miss six-to-eight weeks but wound up missing essentially the entire season. At one point, the doctor said I needed a knee replacement and I should retire, but later acupuncture allowed some blood flow back in my knee, which helped to restore muscle and take the pressure off my joints. I'd originally gotten hurt in Atlanta two weeks before the playoff series with the Chicago Bulls the season before. I wasn't supposed to play that series, but I toughed it out, even though my knee was reduced to bone-on-bone. Then I had to pay for putting off surgery. And to be quite honest over the course of that year, I learned to despise crutches. I'd used them since August after my knee surgery, and they just always hurt my armpits. I only played in six games and only a total of about 75 minutes. It was obviously nowhere near my standard. I hated that more than I can say. But I didn't want to complain about anything to anyone. Not my surgery, not basketball, not my separation (and eventual divorce in 1997) with Kim, not my crutches. In many ways, like me, the Hornets franchise was at a crossroads, too. We'd lost Mourning and we had a bunch of new faces in the locker room. In the trade for Zo, we acquired Glen Rice and Matt Geiger and the second-year guard, Khalid Reeves, who would help our bench.

Rice fit in great with L.J. He could score on the perimeter and shoot the lights out. He was a 6'7" deadeye, which helped to stretch the floor and give Johnson more room to use his strength and operate on the inside. Geiger was a nice compliment to the roster, too. He could get a few buckets when we needed them, but he wasn't the type of player who needed plays designed for him. He was a solid defender and great on the boards. I didn't want Zo to leave, of course, but we got some good players back for the Big Fella. It was hard to see Hersey Hawkins and David Wingate go, too, but it was great to get Kendall Gill back on the roster. He was a good fit in Charlotte, but he never seemed to stay put for too long with us unfortunately. After less than half the season, Gill was traded again to the New Jersey Nets in January, along with Reeves, for veteran point guard Kenny Anderson. Because of my injury, the Hornets had to find another floor general, and Anderson was the guy. He'd been an All-Star in 1993–94 and he was in the last year of his contract that season so the team had flexibility after the season once I got my knee right.

Anderson could score and pass and was quick like a fox. He had come into the league in New Jersey with such promise, along with the power forward, Derrick Coleman, but neither had totally lived up to the massive hype. But Anderson definitely helped our team that season, and I was grateful for that, even though I was frustrated to be sidelined. I never want to sit by and let my teammates do all the work. To begin the year, we got off to a slow start, losing eight of our first 11 games. We hovered around .500 for much of the season with a patchwork backcourt. That year we could never seem to get healthy. It seemed like before each game, the coaches would tell us someone different was out. Our talented wing, Scott Burrell, was out for much of the season with a shoulder injury. The poor guy could never seem to be at full strength. But the worst fell on Johnson.

L.J. was still playing through terrible back pain. He gutted through and played 81 games that year, which was remarkable given the pain he dealt with. In those games he averaged 40.4 minutes, 20.5 points, and 8.4 rebounds per contest. He was a hero for us, especially in Zo's absence. That season it was difficult not to scoreboard watch the Miami Heat. I didn't want to take part in it, but I found myself checking what Zo was doing on his new team. They'd traded a lot to get him and weakened their roster as a result. That season Mourning averaged 23.2 points and 10.4 rebounds a game, and the Heat improved vastly from their lackluster year before. The Heat finished 42–40. But it killed me that our team finished just one game behind them despite losing our best player.

Our record at the end of the year was exactly .500. We finished 41–41 and missed the playoffs by just *one* game. If there was a silver lining, it was that we led the league in attendance yet another year. The fans hadn't given up on us despite injures and Mourning's departure. Rice had a great year. He was an All-Star and averaged 21.6 points and shot 42.4 percent from three-point range. Curry played well, too, averaging 14.5 points per game, playing all 82 games, and shooting 40 percent from three. Anderson was excellent, averaging 15.2 points and 8.6 assists in 38 games for us after playing 31 for the Nets. But in the summer again there was a lot of player movement.

Anderson was a free agent and he signed with the Portland Trail Blazers to be their long-term starter. Robert Parish had completed his two-year contract with us and he opted to sign with the Bulls. But those weren't nearly the most significant moves for the team in the offseason. Just a year after losing Mourning to Miami, the Hornets front office traded Johnson to the

New York Knicks. It was devastating. Next, coach Allen Bristow stepped down. Just like that, seemingly overnight the whole organization felt different. During the season I'd worked all year to get back, rehabbing my knee, studying tape, working with the young guys, and our foundation suddenly walked out the door. Johnson hadn't been happy much of the season; I knew that. He felt he carried too much of the team's burden and he was constantly playing hurt. So the Hornets ended up dealing Johnson to the Knicks for the rough and tough left-handed power forward Anthony Mason. I was sorry to see my good friend go. It hurt, to be honest.

To replace Coach Bristow, the front office hired Dave Cowens, a former NBA MVP, Rookie of the Year and player/coach on the Boston Celtics. Cowens was an accomplished NBA figure and cared about offense. I knew we could work well together. I tried to keep a positive attitude through it all. Nevertheless, everything felt pretty surreal. I knew the NBA was a business, and transactions like these happen all the time. But, for me, it seemed like Zo, L.J., and I would play together for 10 years and make it to a few Finals at least. Did business have to get in the way of that? After just three years, that was all gone. The three amigos? *Poof.* We didn't have a long enough run together if you ask me. We left a lot of wins and a lot of lob passes on the table.

Once Johnson was gone, a new reality hit, and I was curious how the front office was going to improve our team for the upcoming season. Mason was a good player and playoff tested. He wasn't a franchise guy like Johnson, but he was very, very good in many facets of the game. He was strong on defense, a skilled passer, and a no-nonsense presence on the floor. He'd fit in well for the upcoming 1996–97 campaign. I'd seen him in many battles with the Knicks, getting in scuffles with his opponents, protecting Patrick Ewing. I liked that. Toughness is good on the basketball court, especially if talent accompanies it hand in hand.

During the draft the Hornets also made one of the biggest trades in NBA history. It was controversial at the time. When you look back on it, the fate of the league changed that day. Of all the moves that offseason, the trade the Hornets made with the Los Angeles Lakers was definitely the most monumental. No one knew it at the time (well, maybe the Lakers' executive, Jerry West did), but that trade would affect the future of basketball for decades. On July 11, 1996, the Hornets sent the rights to the 13th pick in the 1996 NBA Draft to Los Angeles for the veteran center Vlade Divac. Of course, Divac was a good player, who started on some great Lakers teams with Magic Johnson. He could rebound and pass with the best of 'em and he brought experience and a good personality to the locker room. In many ways, we'd upgraded for the season. In Divac's seven seasons with L.A., he averaged 12.5 points, 8.7 rebounds, and 2.6 assists per game. In his first season for us, he even outdid those averages.

But the only problem with the whole trade was that the 13th pick in that year's draft turned out to be Kobe Bean Bryant, the 17-year-old shooting guard from Lower Merion High School in Philadelphia! Bryant, of course, became one of the greatest and most accomplished players in NBA history before his untimely death in 2020. In that trade the Hornets made a win-now move in acquiring Divac, and we appreciated that. The team didn't want to wait around on what they saw was a developing rookie. We had veterans who could make waves now. A lot of experts had talked up the quality of the 1996 draft. It was one of the most celebrated. Three of the next four picks after Bryant were Peja Stojakovic, Steve Nash, and Jermaine O'Neal. All three of those guys were All-Stars, and Nash is a two-time MVP. Ahead of them was Allen Iverson, Ray Allen, and many other greats.

But getting Divac also made sense for us. At the time size was at a premium, and we needed help in the middle. Geiger was strong, but he couldn't play the whole game. The Lakers valued Divac, but he was quickly made available because the team had Shaquille O'Neal coming in from the Orlando Magic as a free agent. Officially, the Shaq and Kobe era had started. It may have taken a few years to get going at full speed. (Bryant only averaged 7.6 points his rookie season.) But the duo would famously go on to win three championships together from 2000 to 2002, and Bryant would go on to win two more with L.A. before he retired. It's hard to imagine what Bryant would have become on the Hornets had he not been traded. So much about an NBA career arc is about fit, where a player lands. Bryant in so many ways *was* the Los Angeles Lakers: the glitz, glamour, and intrigue.

It's easy to picture Bryant's photogenic, recognizable face right now with his big aviator sunglasses and toothy Hollywood grin. This is, of course, not to say that Kobe would have been worse in Charlotte with me, Rice, and Mason. A player like Bryant can succeed anywhere. Bryant could have easily been the franchise's best player after everything was all said and done, our own facsimile of Michael Jordan. But I wonder if the basketball gods simply never would have let that happen for him in North Carolina. Bryant *needed* to be in L.A., and L.A. *needed* Bryant. You play this game long enough and you begin to see the basketball gods at work in their mysterious ways, keeping a watchful eye over the game like chess masters. The NBA is better when the Lakers are contenders. Everyone knows that.

As the 1996–97 season approached, Curry and I were again the team's veteran leaders, the franchise's original dynamic duo. Dell had met his wife, Sonya, in school at Virginia Tech where he played basketball, and she played volleyball. They'd had their first child, Wardell Stephen "Steph" Curry II, in March of 1988 during Dell's second season in the NBA in Cleveland. Dell and Sonya had their second son, Seth Adham Curry, in August of 1990 after Dell's second year with me in Charlotte. Brittney and Steph used to have little Valentine's Day dates together as kids. Seth and Ty Jr. were friends, too. (They would later be in each other's weddings.)

In fact, there's a funny story everyone remembers when Dell had to dress up in a Barney suit for Seth's four-year-old birthday party. His ankles stuck out, and little Steph asked, "Dad, is that you in there?" Dell replied, "Yes, that's me, son. Now go away and don't tell anybody!"

In October, just before our 1994–95 season, Sonya gave birth to the couple's third child, a girl named Sydel Curry. Kim threw her an epic baby shower that people still talk about to this day.

I'm sure some people hypothesized that the three Curry children would be fine athletes, but no one could have predicted that one would play Division I volleyball, two would make the NBA, and one would become a two-time MVP and the best shooter ever. I still remember little Steph running around on the court with Seth following him. I'd pick those boys up and fly them around like airplanes. As kids and young basketball players, they were little sponges. They always asked questions. No one back then was thinking about the type of players they'd become 20 years later. Steph was never the biggest guy out there, which, of course, I could relate to. But he wanted it more than anyone else. He wanted to get good like his pops. Dell was a marksman shooter, and that skill transferred through the family genes because both Steph and Seth are two of the best ever to do it. Just look at their percentages. But they get their toughness and grit from their mother.

Sonya is a fierce woman and has always been a supportive parent. Dell would tell his boys to ask me about playing point guard since it was their natural position. So, I'd talk to them about how to run a team, how to make an impact on both sides of the court, how to take a hit and finish the layup. As the boys got older, I continued to teach them the game. I showed them veteran moves like what to do when someone is posting you up or how to take the ball from someone dribbling up the court by letting them go by you for a split-second. I taught them how to get space on the court by using their dribble, how to start a fast break, how to keep their heads up and be ready for what the defense gives you. I tried to make the game simple for them so they could get better and maybe one day make the NBA. But I also tried to build their confidence up. I knew they'd hear it all on the playground about being smaller and who their dad was. They had to be mentally tough. That was maybe the most important.

However, even I never thought they'd be *this* good! Steph, who was a gym rat growing up, has won three championships, and I wouldn't be surprised if Seth gets one or two of his own before he hangs it up. It would be great one day if they got to play together. It's odd to think about playing one-on-one with them as kids with Nerf hoops. Steph, who was actually born in LeBron James' hometown of Akron, Ohio, when Dell played for the Cleveland Cavaliers, first began to turn heads when he was in high school at Charlotte Christian. At the time he was a reluctant scorer. His coaches had to instill in him shot *minimums* of five per quarter. That's when people began to talk about him succeeding at higher levels. Still, though, he didn't get any big-time college offers. Virginia Tech, his parents' Alma mater, offered him a redshirt scholarship, but Steph wanted to play right away. The local Davidson University decided to offer him a scholarship, and the rest is history. Steph helped lead Davidson to an Elite Eight. He could have turned his nose up at the opportunity at Davidson, but instead Steph saw an opportunity, and he thrived.

But entering the 1996–97 NBA season, neither Steph or Seth Curry, who would later star at Duke University under Coach K, were quite old enough to fill out a regulation Hornets uniform. They couldn't help us out yet. So it was up to Dell, me, and the rest of the guys. We had our eyes on a bounce-back year. I was healthy and ready to show I could lead this new team. As the season began, we got off to an okay start, playing a little better than .500. After an early January loss to the Phoenix Suns, our record fell to 18–16. But I could feel we were ready to make our move. Around the All-Star break, the Hornets traded Burrell to the Golden State Warriors and acquired guard Ricky Pierce from the Denver Nuggets. Pierce solidified our rotation and filled in for me as our starter if I had to sit out a game or two.

It can take some time for a newly assembled team to gel, and we had a lot of new players like Pierce, Divac, and Mason. But after that January loss to the Suns, we went on a big tear, a hot streak. We coalesced as a squad, finishing the season on a scorching 36–12 run. We were a well-oiled machine. While many of the faces were new on the roster, the foundational habits we'd laid over the years as a franchise held true for the year. We were a team to take seriously. I knew that each time I touched the ball, I had to push, push, push up the floor. I wanted to get out in transition and set up Rice or Curry on the wing or Geiger, Divac, or Mason around the basket for a dunk. With each fresh possession, I wanted to pressure the defense. Get them on their heels, then strike with one of our many scorers.

When you have guys who can finish, the point guard's job is much easier. That winning streak took our final record to an all-time franchise high 54–28. Expectations going into the season were low, and we'd vastly exceeded them. Coach Cowens had done well in his first year, pushing a lot of the right buttons. In a new way, things felt back to normal again. At home Chuckie was with me. We were inseparable. For as much as I'd helped him, he helped me a lot, too. We'd been together ever since my mom called to tell me what he was going through. Chuckie was the constant in my life. I started bringing him along to practices and to games. My teammates loved him, too. Chuckie could get along with anybody, but I didn't talk about him or my family to the press. I was private in that way. It was too soon for me to address anything like that publicly.

Today I can talk about anything in my past. But back then, everything was still raw. Big Mason was named to the All-NBA third-team, and Rice, who'd had the best year of his career, earned All-NBA second-team honors. Rice was also the All-Star Game MVP, setting a scoring record for the third quarter (notching 20 points) and second half totals (24). Over the course of the season, I'd played in 65 games, starting all of them. I averaged 28.9 minutes, eight points, 7.2 assists, and 1.3 steals per game. I even shot my best mark from three-point range at 41.7 percent. Curry averaged 14.8 points per game and shot an impressive 42.6 percent from three. In fact, as a team, we led the NBA in three-point percentage, shooting 42.8 percent. A lot of that was thanks to Curry and Rice. The latter played 79 games and averaged 42.6 minutes, 26.8 points (third in the league), and 4.0 rebounds and shot 47 percent from three-point range (first in the league). Rice was also first in minutes (3,362). Mason was a beast for us that year. He played 73 games and averaged 43.1 minutes (first in the league), 16.2 points, 11.4 rebounds (third in the league), and 5.7 assists, which was a ton for a forward.

In 81 games the seven-foot Divac added 12.6 points and nine rebounds per game, and our second seven-footer, Geiger, who came off the bench, averaged 8.9 points and 5.3 rebounds. We were a solid team with a lot of hope heading into the playoffs. In the postseason we were slotted as the sixth seed in the East and faced the third-seeded Knicks and my old buddy, Johnson. During the regular season, we'd trounced the Knicks 3–1, losing our first game to them 113–86 but beating them in each of the next three 93–86, 113–104 (in overtime), and 99–93. In the playoffs, though, I'd like to say that we put up a good fight against the Knicks and that we took it to them. But the truth of the matter is that we got swept in three pitiful games. We just didn't have it. The playoffs can be tricky. Even though your team can come together looking good in the regular season, the playoffs are a different stratosphere for a new group.

Everything can feel brand new again in awkward ways. We lost the three games by a combined 26 points. In Game One we fell in New York 109–99. Divac had 27 points down low, Rice had 22, I scored 13, and Mason grabbed 13 rebounds. But New York outfought us. The Knicks' taleneted shooter Allan Houston scored 25 points, Johnson had 20, Ewing scored 15 and grabbed nine rebounds. I thought we'd just dust ourselves off. Although we played better in Game Two, we still lost 100–93. Rice went wild in Game Two, scoring 39 points. The Knicks threw everyone they could at him, but Rice was hot from inside and outside. Mason added 13 points and 12 rebounds, and Divac notched 14 and 12. But I contributed nothing. I'm almost embarrassed to say that I couldn't play in the game. I had to sit out with knee soreness, which frustrated me to no end. It was the right call health-wise, but it felt like the wrong one in the moment. I hated to sit. I really wanted to play, but I didn't even get to suit up. I was in street clothes.

In the third and potentially series-clinching game, we were back in Charlotte at The Hive, and I was ready. I started the game and scored 19 points, passing out three assists. It was one of my best playoff scoring games. I was on fire from the field, which also helped set up my teammates. Rice added 22 points, Mason got 14 points with 11 rebounds, and Divac got 13 points. But we just couldn't pull it out. Our defense just wasn't there. The Knicks had seven players who scored in double-digits, and L.J. topped them all with 22 points. I imagined he liked that stat line. Our fans made sure to boo him much of the game. In the final minute, we were down by four points with just 58 seconds left when Johnson hit a big three-point shot for the Knicks, leaving just 44.7 seconds left. It was the dagger.

We lost Game Three 104–95. It was beyond disappointing; it still eats at me today, to be honest. It wasn't how we wanted to go out, especially for our fans who had supported us again for another great year. It's never good to be swept. Coached by Jeff Van Gundy, the Knicks were a physical lineup. Along with Johnson and Ewing, they also had streaky shooter John Starks, muscular forward Charles Oakley, and a guard rotation of Charlie Ward, Houston, and Chris Childs. I hate to admit it, but we got outplayed. We looked up, and it was over. Although we'd outdone expectations for the regular season, amassing the franchise's most victories ever and leading the league in attendance for the eighth time in nine campaigns, we didn't get it done in the playoffs. That's where it matters most.

To win an NBA championship, a team needs tested veterans. But along with that, those veterans need time to come together to really win in the postseason. Rarely does a group of guys do it in their first season together, not even the greatest teams. Yet, losing still hurt. We thought we had a good chance to beat the Knicks. For Mason to lose to his old team and for us to lose to Johnson, that stung. It's the kind of loss that lingers, the kind that sticks with you into the offseason and into the following season. As I walked off our court after we lost to the Knicks, I thought how we'd be back to avenge the loss. But as it turned out, I wouldn't be. At one point in time, George Shinn had promised I'd retire a Hornet. But on November 7, 1997, at the beginning of the new season, the unthinkable happened. I was traded to the Golden State Warriors. I was no longer a Charlotte Hornet.

MEMORY LANE
Kenny Anderson

"In Charlotte, I got to play with some respected players like Glen Rice, Larry Johnson, Robert Parish. We missed the playoffs by one game— because of the Miami Heat, who'd traded for Alonzo Mourning the year before. But overall it was great there; I kind of hoped they would re-sign me. Coach Allan Bristow was an awesome coach. I loved Charlotte for my half a year. And Muggsy was a great teammate. How he got into the league was awesome, him being one of the smallest players to ever accomplish that feat."

13

A NEW SCENE

DURING THE SUMMER BEFORE THE 1995–96 SEASON, THE YEAR I'D SAT out because of my left knee injury, I shot another movie in addition to *Space Jam*. The second movie was *Eddie*. I'd filmed both in 1995 practically back-to-back, even though I was still rehabbing my knee. I'd gotten very familiar with my dang crutches. And both movies came out in 1996. *Space Jam* was a smash hit, and *Eddie*, which starred transcendent comedian Whoopi Goldberg, was a fan favorite, too. Her character, Edwina "Eddie" Franklin, was a limo driver and huge fan of the hapless New York Knicks. She followed every game, heckling the coach every chance she could.

While attending one game after work, Eddie won the chance to coach the team after making a free throw at halftime. And the people of New York, including the team's owner, Wild Bill, quickly fell in love with her charisma, and she stuck around to coach for the rest of the season. It was a pretty wild premise, I'll admit. But the movie was truly great fun. Shooting it also got my mind off my problems at home. *Eddie* featured a lot of NBA players, including Larry Johnson, Mark Jackson, Greg Ostertag, Malik Sealy, Dwayne Schintzius, Vlade Divac, Vinny Del Negro, Avery Johnson, Gary Payton, Anthony Mason, J.R. Reid, Scott Burrell, Hersey Hawkins, Rick Fox, John Starks, Mitch Richmond, Dennis Rodman, and John Salley. It also featured some pretty famous announcers, including Chris Berman, Marv Albert, and Walt Frazier. Fabio and David Letterman made cameos. The conclusion of the movie's plot came down to a final regular-season matchup between the Charlotte Hornets and the New York Knicks. The winner would move on to get the coveted final spot in the playoffs.

Eddie's Knicks beat us after the ref made a bad call on Johnson. Eddie becomes the hero for getting the Knicks to the postseason. When you watch the movie, you can see me on the bench and in the huddle, leaning on my dang crutches. During the filming I told Jackson, who was in the same draft class as I, that I should have been out there to bust him up on the court. It was great fun to work with Whoopi. In fact, she personally asked me to be in the movie, which was an honor. She was a true pro and a cutup in rehearsals. Most athletes want to be actors, and most of the actors that I've met wish they could be athletes. So when you spend time with a person like Whoopi, it's a real treat to see behind the curtain. You see how smart and sharp you have to be in order to be a professional comedian, what it takes to carry a movie. Whoopi had the chops, too. She'd been a comedian for many years. You can't surprise her with anything. Now she's known for her work on talk shows, but back then she was a killer on stage and the silver screen.

I was happy we could share a quick scene together at the end of the movie. It's amazing to see how long a crew takes to set up a scene. Ladders and lights, makeup and stage marking, cameras, and all these takes are needed even for just a few seconds of film. It's a serious process. We shot our scene at The Hive, and I got some extra screen time with Whoopi. That was nice since I couldn't play in the "games." She even flirted with me a bit on camera for a second, and I had a few lines. Even though the Knicks had beaten us in the movie, I actually supported Eddie in her effort to prevent the team's owner from moving the franchise out of New York City. Like I said, the premise was wild! In real life, the Knicks would never leave the Big Apple, but that was the way the story went. But in the end with the Knicks making the playoffs, the city kept the team, and there was a happy ending for everyone (except the Hornets).

Personally, I felt like a big winner. I'd been in two movies that year along with all those commercials and television appearances. People around the country, and in Charlotte especially, were showing my family and me a lot of love. I felt like we'd really found a home in North Carolina and I was ready to stay in Charlotte for years to come. It may seem funny, but when you see your face on a 10-story mural in a city and on T-shirts and busses everywhere, you believe you can plant roots. In the NBA, though, nothing is ever certain, and I should have known that. It's important to be prepared for anything. I can laugh about it now, but it was tough at the time. We really did see our faces everywhere in Charlotte when we were rolling to playoff appearances. Alonzo Mourning, L.J., and I had made big names for ourselves as a trio, and even though we weren't playing together anymore, I still saw us everywhere around the city on jerseys, posters, and old newspaper clippings taped up in barbershop windows.

This was well before social media, and the Internet was only just starting to take shape. But maybe all that should have been a sign that my playing time in the city was nearing its end. L.J. and Zo were both gone. Even though the memory of those years was still fresh, times were changing. In a way it felt like we were a movie cast that broke up after filming despite the fact that everyone wanted a sequel. I was the character the kids loved, L.J. was the guy who wowed everyone with his star presence, and Zo was the blue-collar backbone. We had something for everyone. The whole thing hit a high level with the teal Hornets jackets in the early '90s. By the middle of the decade, those Starter jackets were under nearly every tree by Christmas morning. It seemed as if every kid wanted one of those coats with our big Hornets logo. Those things were just about the hottest item in town for a while. Steph Curry even said, "Whether you were a Hornets fan or not, that was something you wanted to have."

He was right. The teal and purple colors were legendary. The big plastic zipper made the perfect sound when you zipped it up to you chin. There were large pockets in the front and a hood that was perfect for when it rained or snowed during the cold North Carolina winters. The jackets were part of a whole '90s ensemble that went beyond basketball. They were fashion symbols for a lot of people, as strange as that might be. In 1997 Starter began making the jerseys for the Hornets, too. But sadly, I only had two games that year to wear the new look.

Life has a funny way of telling you to slow things down or change things up when you're at the top of your game. There's always another side to the coin, a slope after the high climb. I'd never been more famous as a basketball player, never more comfortable on a team or organization. But that can change in an instant. That's why family is important. I'd taken that for granted and I was paying the price. But I also knew I couldn't let it affect my job as a basketball player.

In 1988 we'd started as an expansion team and built through hard work and the draft to become an annual playoff contender. Now the team had rebuilt on the fly again and was embarking on a new chapter with a new core of Glen Rice, Mason, and Divac to play with me, Dell Curry, and some other veterans. Or so I thought. During the offseason, however, the team had signed talented wing players David Wesley and Bobby Phills. Those guys could score and defend and would be great additions to the team. The Hornets also brought back the team's second ever draft pick, J.R. Reid, to play backup forward off the bench. It was good to see him in camp again. But my dream of playing on the team's new incarnation would never really materialize. Early into the season after I'd played in just two of the team's first four contests, the Hornets traded me and the young guard, Tony Delk, to the Golden State Warriors for veteran point guard B. J. Armstrong. It felt like the team had given up on me.

Honestly, it was a kick to the gut that I wasn't prepared for. But that's life in the league sometimes. The day it happened, Curry came to my hotel room, and we just wept. We hugged one another and knew we'd always be friends, well past our time in the league. But the worst part about it, the real low point, was that the Hornets had lost faith in me as a valuable player. When the organization had signed Wesley, Coach Cowens actually said to the media that he thought I should retire. I thought, *What?* Heading into the 1997–98 season, the team didn't give me much of a chance to compete for the starting job. That felt unprofessional and worse—hurtful, especially since Cowens had only been with the team for a cup of coffee at that point. It felt like the team was broadcasting to everyone in the NBA that I was finished. When I first got word of the trade to Golden State, I thought it couldn't be true. Then my head wondered about the idea of moving coasts and what would happen with Chuckie? I knew I had to move 3,000 miles from my home after giving everything to the team for nine full seasons.

I'd gone through the summer in Charlotte preparing for the new season, rehabbing and strengthening my knee in the gym. I was feeling the love from the movies and ads, seeing the purple and teal everywhere, and now it was time to pack up? But sometimes your first reaction isn't the best reaction. I tried to take a deep breath and have faith. In times of doubt, that can be the most important thing to remember. I was going to have to learn a whole new system and mesh with a new set of players, coach, and management. To be honest, I thought I'd retire as a Hornet and maybe end up in the team's front office. I was sad to see everything turn out this way. It was even worse that there was a bad breakup in the air. I couldn't believe what Cowens had said to the media. I knew I had years left in me. I tried not to show my emotions in the press, but I was angry. You want to believe there is loyalty in sports, especially if you're the face of the team for a decade.

But it doesn't often work out that way. I knew that I missed a year in 1995–96 due to injury, but I also knew that I could still help the team win and maintain my role in the community as an important voice. But no, I was traded to Golden State, and it broke my heart. There was a changing of the guard—literally—and I had to accept it. But I've always been resilient. More than my speed, my tenacious defense, or my ability to find someone on a fast break, my ability to bounce back stronger after adversity has always been my signature. It began on the Baltimore playgrounds and it would continue in Oakland. It felt good to be wanted by Golden State after all. The team's general manager, Garry St. Jean, told *The Baltimore Sun* after the trade, "He may have had a sore knee, but you can't measure the size of his heart." That felt exceptional to hear.

As I began to mentally accept the trade from Charlotte, I began to think about my new team and my new home. How would I fit in? What did they want me to bring? I tried to remember what I knew from playing the Warriors. East Coast teams only play West Coast teams twice a year in the NBA—one home and one away game. But from their logo to their personnel, the Warriors were going through a change at that time. I knew my questions would be answered soon enough. For now, I needed to plan out my next steps. I had to figure out how I would make the transition from the mid-Atlantic to the West Coast. I wasn't certain about how Golden State wanted to use me going forward, if I was going to get a contract extension, or what was next for me. After you get traded once, it's easy to feel like it can happen again and again. I didn't know what my future looked like at this point.

But Chuckie said he wanted to come with me. So, together we went west. I promised my kids I would call them every day. They were growing up before my eyes, and I felt sad to miss out on some of their most important years. Tyisha was a teenager, and Brittney was almost there. Ty Jr. was getting close to double-digits and already playing basketball well. He had dreams of the NBA. I loved when the kids came to games and got a chance to hang out with me on the court and meet my teammates. I would miss all of that. I wished they could come with me, but it wasn't fair to uproot their lives. I would also miss popping up in their classrooms when they weren't expecting me. Tyisha said I would always embarrass her because people would always ask me for autographs. But it was important for me to know their teachers and keep on top of their classwork, even from a distance.

If you're an NBA parent, that means you're often away from your family, but you can still be in constant contact with the lines of communication open. Later, once I got settled, I knew the kids would come out to visit. Brittney and Ty Jr. even learned to play street hockey in Oakland, which was big out there at the time in the late '90s. I knew I would miss the Currys. We'd spent nine years together with the Hornets—from the black-tie opening night (and 40-point drubbing), to beating the vaunted Boston Celtics, to about a million assisted three-pointers, and raucous cheers from the fans at The Hive. But when you have friends like Reggie Williams or Curry, you know you'll always be in each other's lives. It's the type of friendship that you can pick up right where you left off when you see the person again. And I knew I'd seem them all again soon.

I'd often enjoyed my stay on the rare games we'd played Golden State. But I didn't know a lot about the area. The Warriors had a lot of young players they were hoping to develop with a mix of veterans trying to prove they still had what it took to stay in the league. But while the Warriors team was in flux, so was my life. In my quiet moments, I wondered what the trade away from Charlotte meant for me. The fame and my connection to Charlotte was largely in the rearview mirror, but a lot of good basketball was still ahead of me. My resolve to continue my journey felt stronger than ever. Despite the team giving up on me, I'd set my fair share of Hornets records by the time they traded me. When I left I was the NBA's all-time leader in assist-to-turnover ratio and I was the Hornets' all-time leader in minutes played (19,768), assists (5,557), and steals (1,067). I was in the top few in many other statistical categories, including games played (632, second only to Curry), total field goals, and total points. It goes without saying: I was no slouch for the franchise. In fact, it felt great to have left my mark on the team in so many important categories. I knew the numbers would remain in the team record books for years to come. Some of them still stand today, I'm proud to report.

When something important ends, we're faced with a choice: we can either live in the hurt forever or we can cherish what we had and move on. As time went on, I began to embrace the latter. Things began to fall into perspective in my mind better as I let go of my anger from the trade. Time has a way of healing most wounds. I was glad for it. I'd had four great years with Johnson and three with Mourning. I'd gotten to play with Curry nearly my entire career (and I would again soon). I'd been saved from Washington and my experience with the Bullets thanks to expansion and I'd been given a chance to start on an important playoff team for multiple years. I'd set records, had my face plastered on buildings, T-shirts, movie posters, and commercials. What more could anyone ask for? Coming from the Lafayette projects, getting shot at five, losing my father and Reggie Lewis—life can remind you how hard it is over and over. But I'd had a tremendous life in Charlotte. The dream was over, yes, but maybe it was time to dream another one.

* * *

The game of basketball was invented in Springfield, Massachusetts, on a rainy winter day in 1891 by Canadian physician Dr. James Naismith. The sport, which has grown ever since, has done so much for me. If you think about it, basketball is one of the most equitable games on Earth. Anyone can play; that's important. There are hoops in nearly every town in America (and in much of the world). All you need is a ball. You can play by yourself, with one another person, or with several others. To get better at the game, you don't even need a hoop. You can practice dribbling or passing against a wall. That's what I did many days. I dribbled up and down hallways, staircases. I dribbled through my legs and around my back. One hand and then the other. But I never practiced dribbling two basketballs at once. For me that's a no-no. In a game you only dribble one, so I've always thought that's how you should practice. Put the ball out in front of you and move with it backward and forward. Practice protecting it. Dribbling is a crucial part of the game that's too often overlooked. Just imagine a defender like me trying to get the ball away from you. How would you protect it?

When Dr. Naismith invented the game, he couldn't have had any idea what his invention would become more than 100 years later. At first, basketball was invented just to give his gym class something to do as it poured outdoors in the Massachusetts cold. He was an instructor at an early YMCA in Springfield and he wanted his students to remain active, even though they couldn't go outside. So, he nailed a peach basket to a mezzanine balcony, and the game was born. At first they kept the bottoms of the peach baskets, and someone would have to retrieve the ball with a long stick.

The game's first stars were center George Mikan and guard Bob Cousy. Then Bill Russell came in from the University of San Francisco and changed everything. He won 11 rings in 13 years with the Boston Celtics. In a way everyone has been chasing Russell ever since. He set the ultimate standard. Other greats came into the league like Kareem Abdul-Jabbar, Julius Erving, Magic Johnson, Larry Bird, and, of course, Michael Jordan. In the '90s we were all in Michael's long shadow. We pushed him in the regular season and playoffs at our peak, but he always came out as the top dog. He had great teams with players like Scottie Pippen, Horace Grant, and Dennis Rodman, not to mention people like Ron Harper, Steve Kerr, and John Paxson and he always had the same Hall of Fame coach on the sidelines: Phil "the Zen Master" Jackson. They were dynamic together and understood each other. Together Jordan and Jackson were great for the game and for the NBA's rising popularity.

Jordan came back from his baseball stint in 1995, and in 1996 the Bulls beat the Seattle SuperSonics in six games. In 1997 the Bulls beat the Utah Jazz in six. That left the Bulls looking for their second three-peat in eight years, which hadn't been done since Russell's Celtics in the 1960s. Heading into the 1997–98 season, the Charlotte Hornets must have thought they had a shot to stop Jordan from achieving that ultimate goal because the team brought in B. J. Armstrong, one of his former teammates, to replace me at point guard. Armstrong, who was making $2.6 million that year (compared to my $1.8 million), had played with the Bulls for the franchise's first three-peat in 1991, 1992, and 1993. Maybe the Hornets front office thought he would be the key to unlock a series against the Bulls in the playoffs if it came down to it. Truthfully, I didn't know. But they brought Armstrong in and shipped me out west.

But don't get me wrong: Armstrong was a really good basketball player and solid starting point guard. He had a great career in the league and has gone on to succeed off the court, too. If someone was going to fill my shoes on the Hornets, he was as good as anyone to do it. I have no ill feelings toward him. I was upset with the Hornets. When the new season began, I wasn't healthy. I'd hoped to round into shape as the first few weeks of the season progressed. But I was only able to play in two of the Hornets' first handful of games. I came off the bench in both and played a total of 16 measly minutes. I scored six points and got four assists and two steals in the two games. There wasn't much of an opportunity to prove myself before the team sent me to Oakland. But the Hornets had made up their mind, and I was out of their plans.

When I got to the Golden State Warriors a few days later, I was excited to help the team in any way I could. My Warriors career had begun, and I was ready for the new chapter. Change is hard, but it's easier if you're able to accept the new situation and do your best. You have to reinvent yourself. That's part of aging and being a mature adult. I wanted to meet everyone immediately. It's important for me to get to know my teammates and the coaches as much as possible. As a point guard, knowing the personalities, the likes and the dislikes of the people you're working with, can be crucial. Knowing where a player wants to catch a pass in transition or where his sweet spot for a jump shot is on the court can go a long way. We had a lot of talented players on our squad, and I got to know some of them pretty well. The problem was as a team we just weren't very good. We didn't have much chemistry, and Golden State as an organization was in a big state of transition.

Before I got there, the Warriors began the season 0–4. It was a bad year for the franchise and it was only made worse by one of the NBA's most notorious player/coach fights in league history. Less than two months into the season, the Warriors' best player by far, Latrell Sprewell, physically attacked and choked our head coach, P. J. Carlesimo. It happened on December 1, 1997, just a week or two after I arrived in Golden State. And I was right there in the middle of it when it all went down. I couldn't believe my eyes as it happened. The team was in the middle of a losing streak when Coach Carlesimo approached Sprewell and me during a shooting drill. We were in the middle of a rapid-fire exercise, and Coach came over to Sprewell and said, "Put something on the *fucking* pass to Muggsy!"

Sprewell and I looked at each other, puzzled. Spree told him, "I'm tired of you coming at me disrespectfully!"

Coach then kicked him out of practice, and that's when Spree grabbed him and had his neck. I don't know how much pressure he had around his neck. Coach Carlesimo never reached up and grabbed his hands to take Sprewell's hands off him. But you could see Coach's face turning red. (I figure every White person's face turns red when you put your hands on their neck.) Then all of a sudden, everybody came and broke it up and we were able to get them apart. Afterwards, Coach brought us back in and asked if we wanted to resume practice. We all said yes because we'd lost by 40 not that long before. Then we go start practice again, and all of sudden—bam—Spree comes busting back up in the gym. But thankfully nothing happened more than that. Cooler heads prevailed, and that was the extent of it.

We previously got crushed by the Los Angeles Lakers, and I think in that moment both men, leaders of the team, were frustrated. But Sprewell more specifically had simply just had enough. He'd heard enough yelling at him. Coach Carlesimo had been on his back the whole season. In a way, Coach must have thought he was motivating Sprewell. But you have to know your players and know their limits. In that moment Sprewell snapped. At the time Sprewell was our three-time All-Star. He was one of the best 10 to 15 players in the league. Through our first 14 games, he averaged a team high 21.4 points. We needed him. But it was like a volcano blew up.

To make it in the NBA is one of the most difficult things in the world. Sometimes people forget all that it takes to find a place in the game at the highest level. As players there's a lot we have to try to put out of our minds in order to stay focused. But if we let up, it can be an explosion of blind rage. I would never condone what Sprewell did, but I also understood his deep frustration. He was my friend. I was sad to see him suspended for the season. The next day in the press conference, the cameras took video of Coach Carlesimo's bruised neck. The whole thing was awful, beyond dismal for the two men involved and for the rest of the franchise. To be honest, I really liked both guys and was hurt to see them at such violent odds with each other. I knew it would stay with Sprewell his whole career unfortunately. Later that summer he was traded from the Warriors to the New York Knicks. He joined up with Larry Johnson and the rest of the talented team.

I was happy he had a good landing spot, but I wished all of that mess had never happened, and we could have continued to play together in Oakland as a backcourt. We could have built something special potentially. The awful event put the team, which already was fighting an uphill battle, at a further disadvantage. We couldn't come back from it. Yet, we had to keep playing the rest of the season. We wanted to put on a show for our fans and prove there was hope for next season. Oakland fans have always been some of the best in the league, and we didn't want to let them down. Even though I was the new guy in town, I knew we had a responsibility to them. Oddly enough, after Sprewell was suspended, we rallied for a handful of games. Our pride was on the line in many ways. We wanted to show we weren't a group of bums. We went 6–5 in our next 11 games. It was the most successful stretch of the season by far. It gave us an inkling of hope. But after that, we lost nearly every game we played.

I'd gone on the injury list earlier in the season with the Warriors because of a small tear in my right hamstring. A week after I'd come back, I went on the disabled list again for a short period of time. It was frustrating; I didn't like to be away from the team and I didn't want injuries to start to define my career. I hated to be injured frankly. But every player goes through it at some point in his career. I knew it didn't mean I was done despite what some people were saying in the newspapers. I knew I would come back and finish my contract with the Warriors and earn another in the league. When I got back healthy, I was able to contribute solidly to the team. I was tenacious on defense and I could push the ball and find finishers on the break. In fact, I even eventually became the team's starting point guard toward the end of the regular season.

That promotion felt good, and it came during a time when I felt both some doubt in my body and was quite homesick. I got another boost when in a February game against the Knicks in New York, I hit a turn-around, left-handed hook shot over John Starks to win the game in the late fourth quarter. After a free-throw battle, we won 87–82. After the game Knicks legend and sage voice Charles Oakley said, "Littlest man on the court made the biggest shot."

As a team we'd won a total of just eight games before the All-Star break and only 11 more after it. One of the low points of the season was when we lost on March 2 at The Hive to the Hornets. We got blown out actually by the score of 112–83. The fans that night, though, gave me a standing ovation in my first trip back, which I really appreciated. It still hurt not to be there full time.

Halfway through that season, the Warriors had made several more player transactions. Along with the addition of me and Tony Delk early in the year, the Warriors sent out veterans Brian Shaw and Joe Smith to the Philadelphia 76ers and got back guard Jim Jackson and forward Clarence Weatherspoon. The team wanted to shake things up on the roster, and both Jackson and Weatherspoon were good scorers. The Warriors also acquired backup wing Jason Caffey from the Bulls. We already had two solid big men that season in center Erick Dampier, who the team acquired from the Indiana Pacers earlier in the summer, and the sharp-shooting forward, Donyell Marshall. I liked to play with Marshall. He and I had great chemistry on the court. He told the newspapers that, too. He was a friendly face in the new digs.

I was beginning to adjust to my new role on the Warriors. But by the end of the year, we were 19–63 overall, which was one of the worst records in the league. I still tried to put on a show when I was in. Fans loved when I got a steal or hit a buzzer-beater before halftime. But if we hadn't won our last three otherwise meaningless regular-season games, we would have been one of the worst in the NBA's history. I'd endured a few losing seasons before, but those were expansion teams with a roster patched together by new management and first-time team personnel. This felt different. But it was also something I wanted to help turn around. I was thankful Golden State wanted me and I was there to help. I'm not a quitter. I liked many of my teammates and the people running the team. While I was in Golden State, I wanted to win. I had another year on my contract, so I knew I'd be back to work next year, too.

I'd had a good year despite the trade. I'd started 31 of my 59 games with the Warriors and averaged 26.3 minutes, 5.8 points, 5.5 assists, and 1.1 steals per game. In fact, I'd led the team in assists. But perhaps more importantly, I was there to help rebuild the franchise's psyche. An event like the one between Sprewell and Coach Carlesimo can feel like hitting rock bottom. It was up to veterans like me to soften that blow and to help us bounce back to rebuild the team's reputation and standing in the league. Historically, the team has always been strong over the decades. The Warriors franchise, which is now Steph Curry's team, was founded in 1946—even before the

NBA itself officially began—and started in Philadelphia. The team moved to the Bay Area in 1962. It became the Golden State Warriors in 1971. Through the decades the Warriors have boasted some of the league's most important players, including Wilt Chamberlain, Rick Barry, Jamaal Wilkes, Chris Mullin, Tim Hardaway, Mitch Richmond, Chris Webber, Sprewell, Stephen Jackson, Baron Davis, Monta Ellis, and, of course, Steph Curry, Klay Thompson, Draymond Green, and Kevin Durant.

The team won three championships under head coach Steve Kerr in 2015, 2017, and 2018. But whether they won the title or not, what all those Warriors players learned in their careers was that local Oakland fans are some of the best in the league. Coming from Charlotte where we sold out every game for my entire career, I knew what good fans could mean for a franchise, and even if we were losing, they'd support us. If they stuck with the Warriors in 1997–98, they'd stick with the team through anything. The fans have been treated to a lot of good basketball over the years from the championship-winning Rick Barry team to the Run-TMC team with Hardaway, Richmond, and Mullin; to the "We Believe Warriors" with Stephen Jackson and Davis; to Steph Curry's championship teams.

Thankfully, the fans were supportive of me, along with the team, even though I was a first-year player with the organization. I felt loved by them as soon as I stepped on the Warriors hardwood. While I had to battle through injuries, it helped having them in my corner that first season. In a city where I didn't have my family with me and we weren't winning, I had a whole lot of new friends. While we were bad that season, the Hornets were actually pretty great. Just like that first season when I watched Alonzo Mourning from a distance on the Miami Heat, I couldn't help but keep my eye on what Charlotte was doing that season, too. Part of me wanted the team to be bad, but I also knew that I had a lot of friends on the team, and for them I wanted Charlotte to continue to do well. As it turned out, the team had a tremendous season. The Hornets finished the year 51–31 and made the playoffs. Glen Rice scored 22.3 points per game and was an All-Star again.

The Hornets beat the Atlanta Hawks 3–1 in the first round of the playoffs and faced the Bulls again in the second round. The Bulls beat them 4–1, even though the Hornets won Game Two in Chicago 78–76 after Armstrong hit a late game-winner. Jordan didn't take that one too kindly and he shut the Hornets out after that. That year the Hornets finished *second* in attendance in the NBA without me (I couldn't help but smile at that one), and after the season, Vlade Divac left the team for the Sacramento Kings, and Matt Geiger signed with the 76ers. But then the unimaginable happened again: Dell Curry left Charlotte for another squad. He signed a contract as a free agent with the Milwaukee Bucks nearly 1,000 miles away to play with Ray Allen, Sam Cassell (another great Dunbar graduate), Glenn Robinson, and a number of other solid vets like Terrell Brandon, Chris Gatling, Armen Gilliam, and Tyrone Hill.

In a way, it seemed impossible that we were all no longer part of the Hornets. But, of course, it was bound to happen one day or another. Curry was the original Hornet who was selected for the team before even Rex Chapman and I. He had been the team's first pick in the expansion draft. His absence was a real symbol of a new era in Charlotte and around the NBA. The 1990s were officially winding down. Soon the 2000s would be upon us with whatever new challenges, players, teams, and stories they would offer. In the playoffs that season, the Bulls won their third championship in a row, giving them their coveted second three-peat. Jordan hit the final shot in the Finals over Bryon Russell and cemented his legacy as the game's greatest player ever with a swish. Jordan retired for the second time that summer. Some thought the Bulls organization pushed Jordan and the other significant players and coaches on that team out. I believe Jordan thinks that now, too. We may never know the full details of that whole situation, but it's safe to say that the Bulls were one of the greatest teams ever to do it, and now their dynasty was over.

That summer, however, the league as a whole faced a new challenge. Negotiations over the Collective Bargaining Agreement between the players union and the league owners had stalled. It was a stalemate that threatened the future of the NBA and more precisely the following season. If the league locked out the players, the following season could be cancelled or severely shortened. With each passing day, the situation seemed to get uglier and uglier between both sides. The owners threatened to lock the players out of the new season and to withhold all their salaries as a result. This was bad news. All of a sudden, the 1998–99 season seemed in total jeopardy.

MEMORY LANE
Damian Lillard

"I had season tickets when Muggsy was on the Warriors. Muggsy wasn't the biggest star, but because I was always shorter than everybody, the person that I would always think of was Muggsy Bogues. When I would create a player on *2K*—back in the day when I was playing Sega Dreamcast—I would make my player the shortest that you could possibly be; that was 5'5" in the game. I would make my player the shortest you could possibly be because I thought it was so tight that a player that small could be in the NBA and could hang. Then when he was on the Warriors, I got his autograph. Me and my cousin Fred, we used to love Muggsy because he's so short and he's out there hanging in the NBA. So, it was real cool to see him play for the Warriors."

14
THE LOCKOUT-SHORTENED SEASON

IT WAS YET ANOTHER COMPLETELY NEW EXPERIENCE. THE THREAT OF a lockout loomed over the offseason and potentially beyond. Suddenly, whether or not I would play out the final year of my contract with the Golden State Warriors was now in serious doubt, which meant the end of my career potentially hung in the balance, too. I didn't want to think about that nor did I like the idea of sitting out the entire 1998–99 season. But as a member of the NBA Players' Union, I knew I had to stick to the union leadership's decisions. At the same time, it was hard to watch our leaders like Billy Hunter and our team owners stand so far apart on a new agreement. The contract between the owners and players ran out after the season, and we had to come to an agreement before a new season. Labor battles and money discussions can get ugly, and this was no different. As the days progressed, I held out hope there would be a resolution.

Officially, the lockout started on July 1. It was actually the third lockout in the league's history. The disagreement was, of course, over money. The players wanted higher guarantees for minimum salaries, and the owners wanted a bigger share of the total revenue pie. I tried not to think about it too much from a day-to-day perspective. For me one of the highlights of the summer was that Ty came out to stay with Chuckie and me after his school year ended. Following in my footsteps, he was becoming quite a good student and basketball player. Ty and I are a lot to like. We have many of the same traits. Today he's like my best friend. When he came out to Oakland, he stayed with us for about six weeks. I've always appreciated that I can introduce my children to new parts of the world. Seeing how other people live is very important.

As the lockout continued, I flew home to Baltimore with Chuckie to see our family. Most people thought the lockout would last a few weeks, maybe a couple of months. But when it stretched into the next calendar year, a lot of us became more worried. No one wanted the season to be cancelled. It's true that the NBA is a business, but at heart we're all basketball players who want to play the game we love every day. It's a privilege, and we all wanted to be out there. But we wanted it to be fair, too. I wasn't at the center of the discussions, but as an 11-year veteran, I did have a lot of experience with how the league worked at that time. I was lucky as a veteran that I had enough money saved up from my years in the league to feel comfortable about my future. As a result, I could afford to wait out the negotiations. In fact, I took that time to fulfill a promise I'd made to my mother. During the lockout I finished my degree at Wake Forest and got my diploma in communications. My mom was very happy with me for that one. I was the first person in my immediate family to get a college diploma and I had to make her proud.

As the lockout continued, I began to feel bad for some of the younger players. In some ways they weren't prepared for a long stoppage, and that's what the owners used against all of us. In the end the owners got a bigger slice of the basketball financial pie, and we got our increased minimums. The league and our many representatives agreed on a start date for the new season. I think we all breathed a sigh of relief after that. If it had taken any longer, the fans may never have come back to the game. The 1998–99 season did go on, even though it was a rushed, shortened 50-game year. The longer your career, the more you realize how there are fewer and fewer seasons ahead of you, how there is always less time.

The union and owners signed the agreement on January 6, and the new season was slated to start February 5. Normally, the NBA season starts in October, so to start it in a new calendar year felt odd to begin with. But there were a number of other reasons why the season felt surreal that year. I still wasn't completely used to being on the Warriors. I missed my family across the country. The season was shortened, which in some ways felt good, but in others felt awkward and stunted. I was so used to the day-in, day-out grind of a full season. Also, because it was 1999, the whole calendar year felt off. There was the constant threat of Y2K, which I didn't really go for, but everyone kept talking about in the news. There was the wonder of what the new millennium would bring to the world. But the cherry on top of all of this in terms of the league was that Michael Jordan was no longer playing.

We'd finally come back from a lockout, and the league's best player had stayed retired. Now the championship was that much more up for grabs, and everyone in the league knew it. In the offseason the Warriors had made two big moves to get better. In the draft the team used the fourth pick to select the young superstar, Antawn Jamison, from the University of North Carolina. He was regarded highly around the league, and many thought he would be a perennial All-Star. That year Jamison went on to have a good season, portending an even better career. As a rookie he averaged 9.6 points per game, starting in 24 of them. Later, as his career progressed, Jamison quickly blossomed into a perennial 20-point per game scorer. But even more significant than that, just a few weeks before the start of the season, the team finally traded Latrell Sprewell to the New York Knicks.

In return the Warriors acquired Terry Cummings, Chris Mills, and John Starks. From a talent perspective, New York got the best player by far, to be completely honest. But the team had no choice really. Sprewell couldn't come back after putting his hands on P. J. Carlesimo, and Carlesimo was still the team's head coach. The Warriors did the best they could and brought in some good veterans who were fine players and solid for the locker room. In a way the team had started to feel like my early years with the Charlotte Hornets all over again. We were at the beginning of something and we had to build it now brick by brick. It would take patience and work to keep the team chemistry afloat. It would take good drafting and player development. It was a long haul. But if we did it right, it would work and feel great when it crested.

We were a better team in my second season in Oakland—thankfully. Coach Carlesimo preached defense, and we worked hard at it. We weren't the most offensively prolific team in the league, but we grinded defensively and made our opponents work for all of their points. It was grueling to play such a compact schedule. When you're a team in transition and still looking for footing, it can be that much harder to play in uncharted territory. We didn't have years of chemistry together under our belts. So, we started the season sloppy, losing our first five games by a combined 47 points. In our fourth game, we lost a close one 89–82 to the Seattle SuperSonics. I scored four points but notched 12 assists and five rebounds in 32 minutes as the team's starter for that game. We lost a couple more close ones and a few blowouts after that. It wasn't pretty. But we were competing, working. We were trying in good faith, and that meant small, incremental improvements.

Slowly but surely, we started to gain momentum as a unit together. We started to gel as a decent team. We had our pride and we weren't going to be anyone's laughingstock. After our first five losses, we won six of our next seven games. That brought a good mood to the locker room. The energy lifted right along with our spirits. We were having fun again. We remembered why we'd signed up for the league to begin with. Winning is a great medicine, a balm. Young guys like Jamison, Donyell Marshall, Erick Dampier, Tony Delk, and Jason Caffey were learning how to contribute from veterans like me and Cummings. Even Starks, who I'd battled against in the Eastern Conference for years, was fitting well into the team concepts. Starks was our full-time starter on the wing and he played well, averaging 13.8 points per game. I knew he missed the Big Apple like how I missed Charlotte. That's, of course, part of the NBA life.

Other than Cummings' 16 years of service, I had the most NBA experience on the team. The young guys would often ask me for advice about how to succeed in the league day to day, what to do with their paychecks, what to do on the road, etc. I told them to save money and be in bed by curfew. But I also let them know that they could talk to me about whatever they needed along the way. My door was always open. I knew that was part of my role as a veteran on the Warriors. I liked getting to know the guys, and as the shortened season progressed, it helped. We started to play well. We strung some wins together. In the NBA any team can win a single game. But consistency is the goal. If you took away our first five games, which were all losses, and our last five games, four of which were losses, we played .500 basketball for the 40 games in the middle of the season. Not bad, especially after coming off a 19–63 season. That was progress.

We actually won more games in the lockout-shortened year than we had in the full season prior. During that stretch we had some big swings. Some nights we were in control; others we were totally lost. That's the story of a young team. We won some close games, including a one-point nail-biter 91–90 against the Dallas Mavericks in April. And we won some blowouts, too, including one against the Sacramento Kings 114–89 also in April. I ran a lot of the second-team offense and made sure we kept things tight. Overall, we were solid on defense, too, holding teams to 90.8 points per game, good for 12th in the league. I made sure to pressure the other point guards. I averaged 1.2 steals per game, which was slightly up from the year before. Over the course of the season, I played in 36 of the 50 total games, starting in five. I'd actually missed a few due to chicken pox. But I contributed 5.1 points, 3.7 assists, and two rebounds per game.

It was also the first year in my career in which I averaged less than 20 minutes per contest. I'd dipped to 19.8 minutes. Even during my rookie season with the Washington Bullets, I averaged 20.6 minutes. At my peak in Charlotte, I averaged 35.7 minutes per game in 1993–94. Although it's true that Father Time is undefeated as they say, I knew I wasn't his victim quite yet. I knew I hadn't lost a full step. I knew I could still play in the league. While my body—specifically my left knee—wasn't quite the same at 35 years old as it was when I was 20 or 25 years old, I knew my basketball IQ and what I brought to a locker room, a roster, and the court was still top-notch. I had visions later in my career of working in the front office or in coaching. I knew my experience was valuable.

I knew I was still important to an NBA team, especially a developing one. When the season ended, I gave myself some time to decide on my next chapter. In the meantime the playoffs had begun, and I made sure to watch. Even though Jordan hadn't played in the 1994 or 1995 Finals, it always still felt like his spirit was around the game. In both of those years, the Chicago Bulls had played in the postseason, too, and Scottie Pippen had been a beast. But this was the first time that I could remember that Jordan and the Bulls were out of the postseason, a non-factor. There were new stars were at the center of the playoffs. Some of those were Allen Iverson; Shaquille O'Neal and Kobe Bryant; my former teammates Sprewell, Larry Johnson, and Alonzo Mourning; Tim Hardaway; and David Robinson and Tim Duncan. There was a new generation to contend with.

To start the playoffs, the Knicks played the Miami Heat. Both teams hated each other. The rivalry pitted Pat Riley against his former team. It also matched Zo against L.J., and the cold city of New York against sun-kissed city of Miami. It was a battle, but to everyone's surprise, the eighth-seeded Knicks upset the top-seeded Heat three games to two in a bloodbath. The Knicks took that momentum throughout the playoffs all the way to the NBA Finals. To help them do so, Johnson hit one of the most famous shots in NBA history—a four-point play against the Indiana Pacers. The Knicks were down 91–88 with 11.9 seconds left in the fourth quarter of Game Three in the Eastern Conference Finals. He hit a three-pointer, got fouled, and put the Knicks up to win the crucial game. This was all without Patrick Ewing, too. He'd gotten hurt, so he wasn't able to contribute besides waving a towel with his other hand.

Johnson, Sprewell, and the sharp-shooting Allan Houston picked up the slack. They took over in his absence. They put the team and the city on their backs and got all the way to the final series. In those Finals, though, the Knicks met a red-hot San Antonio Spurs team led by the twin towers of Duncan and Robinson along with many other savvy veterans. New York's magic run ran out, and the top-seeded Spurs beat the eighth-seeded Knicks 4–1 to capture the team's first championship in the Duncan era. They'd go on to win four more with Duncan and the now-legendary coach Gregg Popovich. Along the way the Spurs added star players Tony Parker and Manu Ginobili.

Even though the Los Angeles Lakers had lost to Duncan's Spurs that season, their future was also quite bright. In fact, they'd win the next three NBA championships with coach Phil Jackson. Every time I saw Bryant succeed, I couldn't help but wonder what the league would have looked like if he and I were both on the Charlotte Hornets in the late '90s. Every once in a while, I let myself daydream about an ally-oop to Bryant on the break as the fans in The Hive cheered for us. But we both got traded to California. On the East Coast, the Hornets were struggling, too. Always making moves, they'd decided to ship Glen Rice to the Lakers and were working to groom their new big young point guard, Baron Davis, who the team thought would be the future. Funny enough, Davis would have his best days with the Warriors later in his career.

I was a free agent now for really the first time in my long career. I'd signed several contracts along the way in my NBA life but never had I thought I'd play anywhere else outside of Charlotte. I'd always tried to find a deal to stay with the team. Now with my deal up with Golden State, I could theoretically sign for any team. Maybe I'd look to hook up with a developing squad or maybe one who needed a good backup to take them over the top. I knew I would have some interest from teams and an important decision to make. Would I stay with Golden State and continue building? Would I go back to Charlotte? Would I play for Washington again? Would I find an entirely new team: the Knicks with Sprewell and L.J., the talented Lakers? Maybe I'd reach out to Coach Riley in Miami and hook up with Zo?

The future was wide open. But in the end, I knew my best chance was to sign with a young, developing team that needed strong leadership. One of those franchises was the Toronto Raptors. Everyone in the league knew the Raptors had two young and up-and-coming stars in (cousins) Vince Carter and Tracy McGrady. Even though the team was north of the border, they were starting to get national attention. Carter and McGrady could do it all: shoot, jump out of the gym, and take over any game. But they were still very young. To help them along, the Raptors needed veterans, and the team let me know they were interested in my services as part of that growth process. The Raptors needed some experienced players to guide the franchise. That was me.

The organization was also interested in signing my old friend, Dell Curry. I talked with Curry about the idea of us playing together in Canada. I knew that if I signed with Toronto, my family would still be far away but less so. And if Dell Curry was with me in Toronto, that would make the whole situation that much easier. I'd enjoyed my time with Golden State, but I felt *too* far from home. If I played in Toronto, it would be a different country, yes, but it would also be on the same coast and in the same time zone. The team recruited Curry and me to play for the Raptors, and I liked the idea of playing again with one of my best friends. Curry signed about a month before I did, and that solidified my decision. I signed a one-year, $1 million contract on September 23, 1999, to play for the Raptors. I was excited! *Oh, Canada!*

I was headed north with Chuckie on yet another completely new chapter in my basketball career. The game had taken me all over the world. Now, though, reunited with Curry, I knew things would go back to feeling more normal and similar to Charlotte. Our kids could come visit us together. It would feel like a home away from home. And Curry and I could get in rhythm as a backup backcourt duo in Toronto. I also really looked forward to playing with the young Raptors, especially Carter and McGrady. I knew that I was on the back end of my career, but I wanted to finish it on my own terms. I wanted to make the decision when to walk away. In Toronto I could prove my value as a solid guard and perhaps even earn a longer contract after my one-year deal ended. I looked forward to the opportunity. My basketball career had taken me all over the world and now it was taking me to Canada.

NBA players make a lot of money, and we get to play a kid's game for our career and we're all fortunate for that. But there is a price, too. Even though we make good money, it can still be lonely in an apartment or hotel room with your family thousands of miles away. My mom was getting older, too. My dad had been buried for a number of years now, and I was starting to worry about her health. There comes a point when the kids have to start to take care of the parents. I'd worked nonstop on basketball for the last three decades and I could now see the finish line of my playing career. Maybe it would be a year, maybe it would be three or four more. But I was on my third team in four years. It was almost 2000, and I was entering another phase.

MEMORY LANE
Charles Oakley

"We had a ball. We had the best time ever in Toronto. Him and Vince [Carter] got real close. It's amazing when you see a guy like Muggsy. He took fans by surprise. He won them over in Toronto because in Toronto it wasn't about basketball at first. It was a hockey town. But when they saw a guy at 5'3" do what he could do, they said, 'Wow!' He got the whole thing started, him and Vince. In practice Muggsy would always make you better. In the pick-and-roll, he could still turn the corner, get into the paint, and drive. And him and Vince got so many alley-oop plays on fast breaks."

15

AIR CANADA

THE WINTERS ARE COLD IN TORONTO, ONTARIO. THAT WAS THE FIRST thing I had to get used to as I began to settle in with the new franchise. Touching down on a plane and leaving the airport, the chill hits your nose like a frigid flick. The second thing that I had to get used to was my new squad. There was a new offense to learn, new defensive schemes. Ultimately, though, I knew the game of basketball in and out and I wasn't too, too worried about the particulars. For the Toronto Raptors, I also decided to go back to wearing No. 14. I wanted to change from my long-time No. 1 to the number I wore at Dunbar High and Wake Forest. It felt right. We had a great mix of veterans and talented young players. The vets included me and Dee Brown at point, Doug Christie and Dell Curry as the swingmen, Charles Oakley and Kevin Willis at forward, and Antonio Davis, who started for us at center.

But the team revolved around the young Vince Carter and Tracy McGrady. Some people called them the league's next Michael Jordan and Scottie Pippen. For those young Jedi, I would be their Yoda. I wanted to give them advice and help them through their training. Veterans need to show the young stars what it takes to get the proverbial team car keys—namely discipline and hard work. Coach Butch Carter had been with the team for a few years already. He had taken over as the lead guy midway through the 1997–98 season and had helped grow the Raptors ever since. Butch was a former player, and his brother was Hall of Fame NFL wide receiver Cris Carter. Sports were in his family's blood. But Butch was also an outspoken guy who tended to ruffle people's feathers in the process. He had talent on his roster, but he didn't always get along with the people around him. He was good but fiery.

Under him, we started the 1999–2000 season strong. In our first two months, we only lost 12 games and we won 17. Vince was performing like the best player in the league. No one will ever be as good as Jordan, but Vince looked like he might be in the same conversation at times, filling Jordan's high-flying shoes. Vince would go on to play 22 years in the league. That year in 1999–2000, he was our only All-Star. In some ways, playing with Vince reminded me of playing with Larry Johnson. Talk about someone fun to run with. Vince caught one ally-oop I threw to him that was practically behind his head. He plucked the pass from the air, held it in his big palm, and slammed it home with such force that I thought the lights would explode. For the season that year, Vince averaged 25.7 points, 5.8 rebounds, and 3.9 assists. Superstar numbers. But despite all the hype, Vince was a quiet guy off the court.

Vince played flashy like a star, but he didn't want to be the face of the league. It weighed on him. The Raptors drafted him in 1998 (the same year the Golden State Warriors drafted Antawn Jamison) and he was a good rookie right out of the gate. Vince played at UNC (with Jamison) for three years and stood out as one of the best players in the country then. The Raptors drafted McGrady, Vince's cousin, the year prior in 1997. McGrady had come into the league raw right out of high school. The two guys were close. But there was also a little competitive streak between them. They were both so skilled and understandably wanted to be the top dog on their team. But Vince had so clearly established that on the Raptors out of the gate. As the season progressed that year, it felt like McGrady had begun to distance himself from the organization more and more, partly because he wanted to be the top guy and partly because the Raptors and he didn't see eye to eye.

Coach Carter wasn't playing McGrady as much as McGrady wanted or really deserved. Coach wanted to bring him along slowly. But McGrady wanted to make his mark now, and with his talent, he deserved the shot. In January our team went through a rough patch. Yet, somehow we managed a

7–7 record after starting out the month stumbling with three wins and seven losses. We played better into February, winning six of our final eight games before the All-Star break. In one game against the Washington Wizards during that stretch, I came off the bench and played 19 minutes, scoring 11 points and dishing five assists and nabbing two rebounds. Vince scored 26 in that one, McGrady had 20, and Curry added 10. We beat Washington 120–105 to bring our record to a respectable 22–19. A few games later, we beat the Atlanta Hawks 109–88. I played about 24 minutes and racked up six points and 12 assists. After the game I joked with the guys in the locker room, "Still got it!"

During the season McGrady only started about a third of our games. We all knew there was no ceiling to his talent, but he also needed more experience, and that took time. He was rougher than Vince, which was understandable because he'd come out of high school where he'd also focused seriously on baseball and football. (He actually said his first love was baseball.) McGrady finished the year that season averaging 15.4 points, 6.3 rebounds, and 3.3 assists to go along with 1.9 blocks and 1.1 steals. When he dug in, he was one of the best defenders in the league. McGrady could guard anyone on the court. But he thought he should be doing more for us, especially offensively.

In the franchise's fifth year, the Raptors had two players to build on for the future. It was a sign the team was headed in the right direction. In my fifth season with the Charlotte Hornets, we'd drafted Alonzo Mourning and were headed for a win against the Boston Celtics in the playoffs. The Raptors were feeling that same percolating excitement. The 1999–2000 campaign was the team's first winning season in franchise history and the first time the Raptors advanced to the playoffs. We finished the year with a 45–37 record. During the season I played in 80 games, starting in five of them. It was a comeback season for me. I'd signed a one-year contact for the veteran's minimum to begin the year. I'd bet on myself. I knew I could prove my worth in the league as a valuable player again. Now I had. Even though I was 35 years old, I knew if I played well, I would likely earn one more long-term deal. I'd averaged 5.1 points and 3.7 assists for the Raptors and contributed a great deal behind the scenes. I also led the league in assist-to-turnover ratio at 5.07-to-1, which I'd done six other times in my career, and I brought my minutes average up to 21.6. Overall, I was pleased with my performance.

Betting on myself had been smart. The cherry on top was that we made the postseason that year. I was thrilled for the organization, for Vince, McGrady, and Coach Carter. Coach became the first coach in the history of the NBA to take a team with fewer than 20 wins to a playoff appearance in less than two years. He'd done a great job for the franchise and the city as a whole. But behind the scenes, Coach Carter still had trouble getting along with the star players. Vince and T-Mac wanted to play more and freer, especially McGrady. But Coach Carter insisted on limiting their minutes. I could understand both sides of the argument, to be honest. Sometimes there is no real solution to a problem. But there wasn't time to worry about that once the postseason came around. I knew what the playoffs meant for a young team in a new basketball city. It takes a lot of hard work to get to that place, a lot of bumps and bruises along the way.

Former Detroit Pistons point guard Isiah Thomas first led the Raptors, which was originally named after a dinosaur (the velociraptor) made popular by the movie *Jurassic Park*. In 1995 the team's first pick in the expansion draft was B.J. Armstrong, who didn't report and was quickly traded to Golden State. In a funny twist of fate, Armstrong and I would later be traded for each other. The team's first choice in the amateur draft that same summer was Damon Stoudamire, the excellent guard from the University of Arizona. He was a shorter guy for the league, just 5'10", and his nickname was "Mighty Mouse." The next year the Raptors selected the standout center, Marcus Camby, from the University of Massachusetts. He was a skilled defender and a prolific rebounder. With Camby and Mighty Mouse, the team's future looked bright. Nevertheless, the organization struggled for the next few years until T-Mac and Vince came along.

In 1997 the Raptors drafted McGrady, who was still a teenager at the time. In McGrady's rookie season, the team went 16–66, which was one of the league's all-time lowest win totals. But the following year, the Raptors selected Vince and traded Camby to the New York Knicks for veterans Oakley and rookie Sean Marks. The team now had a foundation to build on. "It was a different deal when y'all came to the team," McGrady told me and Oakley.

When I came to the Raptors the following year, along with Curry, we helped to bring much needed depth and experience to the team's backcourt, too. Not only were we all solid veterans, but we also played well with stars and knew how to fit into a team concept. We knew what it took in terms of team chemistry to succeed. The team's overall plan was working, and we were winning games. We were 26–21 at the All-Star break, and that's where Vince truly had his coming-out party. It was his coronation as one of the league's best and most exciting players. Vince's now-famous showcase at the 2000 dunk contest still has people talking.

In the pantheon of great dunk contest participants, there's Jordan, Dominique Wilkins, Spud Webb, Dr. J, and Vince. That's it. That year Vince showed off his amazing jumping ability and his basketball creativity. Vince did reverse 360s, mean-mugged for the camera, dunked from the baseline under the basket, threw down an ally-oop through his legs, and finished by putting his elbow through the hoop like a boss. No one had ever seen that dunk before, including Marv Albert or Kenny Smith, who were excitedly broadcasting the contest for TNT that night. In a way, that was the coming-out party for the entire Raptors organization. The question was whether or not the team would be able to keep it all together and make a push in the playoffs. For some NBA players, Toronto wasn't exactly a desired destination. But everyone wondered if maybe Vince and McGrady would change that trend.

After the All-Star break, we were so hyped from Vince's performance that we trounced the Knicks 91–70 in our first game of the season's second half. Vince averaged 33 points against New York during the regular season. But that wouldn't be the last time we saw New York. They were our opening round opponents in the playoffs. It seemed as if I was always running up against them in the postseason. We finished the season with the team's best record in franchise history. We had toughness, experience, and young stars, and it felt good to be a part of a winner again after two hard years trying to build one in Oakland. I appreciated the process of helping to develop a team. But, really, there is nothing like being a part of a winner. When the playoffs began, we faced the Knicks in the first round. We were the sixth seed, and they were the third—just like the last time I'd seen them in the playoffs with Charlotte. In that series we were swept.

In this one—I'm sorry to say—we were swept, too. We lost to New York in three games. But it wasn't like Latrell Sprewell, Allan Houston, Johnson, and Camby kicked our butts. We only lost by a combined 12 points in those three really hard-fought games. They were all very close. We just couldn't close out any of the games. Although we had some experience on our roster, our young guys were still trying to figure out how to carry us in the postseason. The Knicks, on the other hand, had made the playoffs nearly every year since I'd been drafted. The franchise was a machine. Looking back, we didn't really have any shot. In the series, Vince averaged 19.3 points, and McGrady added 16.7. I played 29 minutes per game, which was fifth on the team. But we just weren't ready to take the next step unfortunately. When a team experiences its first run in the playoffs, the players often have a hard time closing games. We were no different unfortunately.

In Game One at the World's Most Famous Arena, in New York, McGrady was our star, scoring 25 with 10 rebounds. Vince had 16, and I added six points off the bench with an assist, a rebound, and three steals. The Knicks, though, boasted five players in double-digits that day, and they eked it out against us by just four points. We did feel more confident going into Game Two. I started and played 39 minutes. Vince scored 27 points, McGrady scored 13, and I added six with one steal, two assists, and three rebounds. But New York continued its balanced attack. Four of their players scored in double figures, including Sprewell, who dropped 25. We lost by one, 84–83. In the clinching third game, our confidence was shaken. We were boosted by our first home playoff game at the Air Canada Centre in Toronto, but we couldn't pull the game out. New York had another five players in double-digits. Vince had 15 points, McGrady had 12. I started

Game Three and scored four points with two assists and two rebounds. But it wasn't enough.

Although we were up by a point—70–69—with 6:45 left in the game, we lost in the end by seven points, 87–80. We just couldn't close, which was a sign of inexperience. But we weren't the only ones who fell short that year. Only one team ends their season with a win. Also that postseason, the Hornets lost to the Philadelphia 76ers in the first round, and later in the playoffs, the Miami Heat lost to New York yet again. In the NBA Finals, Kobe Bryant and Shaquille O'Neal's Los Angeles Lakers beat the Indiana Pacers, who had Reggie Miller, Jalen Rose, and Mark Jackson, for the first trophy of the Shaq and Kobe era, though it wouldn't be the last. While there was great celebration in L.A., it wasn't quite the same in Toronto. Our loss to the Knicks was hard enough to swallow, but the real pill came during the summer. The franchise had tasted success and now it wanted more.

But some very important, difficult decisions had to be made. Some of those, though, were out of the organization's hands. After the season the Raptors fired Coach Carter despite the playoff appearance. We also lost McGrady to a big free-agent contract with the Orlando Magic. He'd grown up 30 minutes from Orlando, watching the team with O'Neal and Penny Hardaway. That's where he wanted to be, and he also wanted out of Toronto. So McGrady went to go play with All-Star forward Grant Hill. McGrady just didn't get along with management. Some in the media said it was a disagreement between him and Vince, but that was never the case. In the end I couldn't really blame T-Mac. It was his time to see how big of a player he could be. He'd been in Vince's shadow and now he wouldn't be. The following year McGrady became an All-Star, averaging 26.8 points, 7.5 rebounds, 4.6 assists, 1.5 steals, and 1.5 blocks per game, taking over as the Magic's team leader since Hill was injured. Overnight, McGrady had become an NBA superstar, one of the league's 10 best franchise players.

But I'd done in Toronto what I'd come to do. We made it to the playoffs for the first time in franchise history. I'd played an important role. I'd led the team in assists in 16 games, and we had an 11–1 record when I scored 10-plus points. I even matched my career high of 24 points in a win against the Celtics that season. When Curry and I had arrived in Toronto, there were doubts about whether we could play and about whether the team would thrive. We proved all those people wrong. But even more than that, the city of Toronto and all the fans really embraced us. In many ways, it felt a lot like Charlotte all over again. The city embraced me, too. It was a young team in a new city, and I represented something special to the fans. My whole career has always been a success against the odds. Although the goal every year is to advance and win the championship, only one team gets to achieve that each season. So, it's all right to take pride in other gains and victories. We could all feel good about making the playoffs for the first time in franchise history.

But there were still a lot of questions. I'd signed a one-year deal with Toronto and now I was a free agent. I was at yet another crossroads. I'd bet on myself and I had options after a solid year with no major injuries. I didn't have to accept just another one-year deal. I wanted to find security in a long-term contract. I knew I could still play at a high level and I knew my experience in the league was valuable in the locker room. But the league was getting younger.

Yet I knew there was still a role for me in the NBA and I decided to remain with Toronto. So in the offseason, I happily resigned with the Raptors. I put my name to a new four-year deal and, truth be told, I was thrilled. I was happy that I'd retire a Raptor. I felt at home in the city. I loved the fans, and they loved me back. I knew I played an important role in the squad's development. Kids would show up to the games wearing Muggsy Bogues jerseys, shouting, "Muggsy! Muggsy! Muggsy!"

I liked to be someone kids could look up to and I was thankful for the opportunity to come back to the team and be that person. It was tough to be away from home and away from my kids, but Toronto offered me the long-term financial stability I'd hoped for to support my family for years to come. I signed my multi-year deal with the team on September 14, 2000.

When they announced my new contract, Raptors general manager, Glen Grunwald, said I'd played an "instrumental part in a number of our wins" the season prior. He also acknowledged the leadership I brought and how important that was for guys like Vince.

I was glad to stay in Toronto. It's still one of my favorite North American cities. It's big, diverse. There are lots of restaurants and places to visit. Although one of my personal favorite foods is chicken nuggets, Toronto is a city where you want to try the entire food spread that the city has to offer. I love to try different cuisines, and Toronto is perfect for that. The city was my new basketball home, and I looked great in the purple and black jersey. But while I had newfound professional security, my personal life was still very much in flux. I hated that my kids were growing up without me. You can only do so much as a parent over the telephone. All of this weighed on me during the offseason.

Even worse than that, my mother's health was now in serious decline, too. My mother was the most important person to me in my life and to know that she was suffering was in many ways beyond what I could bare as a person. She had cancer, and it seemed like she didn't have much longer to live. I talked with Sherron about what we should do. But no matter how much I tried to plan or figure out the best move for the future, my life would soon change again forever, and it was totally out of my control. When I'd thought about the end of my career, I knew I'd wanted it to come on my terms. When I walked away, I wanted it to be up to me. But I would soon find out that hope would be about as far from reality as possible. As hard as I'd worked and as much as I'd gained in my life, I was about to lose so much more.

MEMORY LANE
Vince Carter

"When you come to a new team, you have to adjust to what the coach has in store for you. But for a young Vince Carter or a young Tracy McGrady, talking to a guy like Muggsy who had so much success in the NBA and at his height, we were all ears. We had a team full of veterans at that time. Most of the teams then were mostly veterans and a few young guys or rookies, as opposed to what it looks like now. So, it was easy for Tracy and me to listen to somebody like Muggsy. He was one of those guys who was always willing to be asked questions. He pointed us in the right direction and told us when we were wrong. That's how I learned how to be a veteran, just from his example of how to be available. I think that's very important, how *there* Muggsy was for us.

"Whenever we had questions or concerns, Muggsy was available and knowledgeable for us to help us through our ups and downs. If you're 5'3" in the NBA and you have that kind of career over 13 or 14 years and you're still in the NBA as the game was changing, at his position he still found a way to be there, to play big minutes. He was respected enough to be there. I was soaking up all the knowledge of any veteran that wanted to help me. Muggsy was like, 'Young fella, let me tell you something.' I was all ears. There was obviously something he was doing right. Muggsy was critical of us, which helped us grow. It was like that from the beginning. He was always in our corner as a point guard. You're a fool if you don't listen to your team's veteran point guard.

"One of my favorite moments with Muggsy in Toronto was against the Milwaukee Bucks. He got the ball at halfcourt and he threw it ahead of me to catch for a windmill dunk. After I dunked he leaned back and spread his arms and yelled out loud. It was organic, unscripted. That moment still makes me laugh."

16

GRIEF

THE 2000–01 SEASON WAS MY LAST IN TORONTO AND MY LAST IN THE NBA as a player. I'd never dribble the ball in the league again. But before the season, I'd signed a four-year contract with the Toronto Raptors. I was hopeful about the organization. The Raptors had made a coaching change, and while I loved Coach Carter, the great Lenny Wilkens was a prestigious replacement. Wilkens would later retire with the most wins ever for an NBA head coach. The franchise also brought in my old draft day pal, Mark Jackson, to play guard with me. Famously, Jackson and a teenage Steph Curry would hold shooting contests at Raptors practices that season. (Jackson would later coach Curry on the Golden State Warriors.) It was shaping up to be a good Toronto team. We had potential and a mix of experience and star talent. I was looking forward to the new year, but that was all immediately dashed. Everything in my personal life was about to shatter again.

My mom's health had suddenly taken a turn for the worse, and she didn't have much time to live. She was battling breast cancer and it was getting to her despite the doctors' best efforts. Kim's father had also been diagnosed with cancer and he was going through it, too. If that wasn't enough, on the court I was experiencing pain in my right knee. So as the season began, I had to sit again. I couldn't play. But once my mother's health became a serious issue, she became my only priority. I left the Raptors to take care of her early in the season. While I thought I might return to the team later on, I never did. Sadly, cancer took my mom, and she was called up to God in November of 2000. My heart fell a thousand stories that day. I knew I couldn't play another game in the league. So, I simply retired. Although I could have played four more seasons and totaled 17, 14 would have to do.

Thankfully, the Raptors were first-class about everything. The team held onto my contract and continued to pay me while I attended to my family and the funeral affairs. In the NBA a contract can be a valuable part of a trade, and since I was no longer playing in the league, my contract might serve the team as an asset to acquire another player. But to be honest at the time, that was the furthest thing from my mind. My mother was my whole world. She was the first person to support me in my life, to love me, to shield me from the jokers, jocks, and jerks. She helped me at every crucial moment in my life. Then she was gone. I had no strength to play basketball. But when it rains, it pours. Around that time, too, Kim's father passed away. They died within two months of each other. Our family was brutalized now. I'm quite sure I wouldn't want anyone to feel that feeling we went through. When I lost my mom, I lost a special part of my own heart.

The only positive was that she'd seen me play my last NBA game. Death is a part of life. But in my life, I've experienced too much of it. In the inner-city of Baltimore, you get too used to death. I saw someone die on a basketball court before I'd even kissed a girl. But nothing can prepare you for your own mother passing away. When she left us, everything in my body felt like it crashed to the ground. I couldn't keep a dry eye at her funeral. At times afterward I could hardly move. I couldn't help but wish everyday she was still with us. But then, of course, life has to go forward. No matter how tough life can be, the world continues to spin. But nothing came easily. Kim and I were still divorced, and she had the kids. She lived in New York for a couple years before moving to Baltimore to start her career with HBO. Although I talked to the kids every day, I didn't see them enough. Distance never makes love easy.

Thank goodness Chuckie was still with me. After leaving Toronto we moved back to my house in Charlotte. After mom died Sherron took over her house, which sat just a few minutes outside of the city. Later that year the Raptors traded my contract to the New York Knicks along with Jackson for point guard Chris Childs and a 2002 first-round draft pick. My agent told me about it, but I was too busy in my own life to pay much attention. I knew I wasn't going back to play in the league. After the season I was traded again in the summer—this time to the Dallas Mavericks. The transaction involved three teams: the Knicks got guards Howard Eisley and Shandon Anderson, the Houston Rockets got my old pal Glen Rice and guard Kyle Hill, and Dallas got me. But since I was long retired, Dallas' new owner Mark Cuban worked out a deal with my agent. Cuban agreed to pay the rest of my salary and at the same time get my contract off the team's official salary cap. He bought me out, even though I'd never played a single game for the Mavericks. I'll always love and appreciate him for that.

Now that my financial situation was clear and covered, I was able to stand back a little bit from my career to appreciate what I'd accomplished. I'd given my heart completely to the city of Charlotte. For the expansion franchise, I'd played a total of 632 career games and I'd started in 80 percent of them. I retired with team records for assists (5,557), steals (1,067), minutes played (19,768), and starts (501). I'd also retired 12th all time in assists and 15th in assists per game in NBA history. (I'm now 23rd.) I accrued five seasons, in which I was top 20 in the league for total steals. I'd amassed 1,369 career steals, which was good for 66th best in league history. In my 14-year career, I finished with 6,858 points, which I was proud of. But I finished with nearly as many career assists (6,726). Few players who'd logged as many minutes as I did could say that. I'd also blocked 39 shots, including one of Patrick Ewing's on April 14, 1993.

In terms of advanced statistics, I finished in the top 20 in offensive rating twice. I was 19th in offensive win shares in 1994–95 and I finished fifth that year in free-throw percentage (88.9). In my time with the Charlotte Hornets, I averaged 10.1 points, 10.1 assists, 3.4 rebounds, and 1.9 steals per 36 minutes. I finished with eight seasons in the top 20 in assists and five in steals. I also accrued six of the top 10 all-time best assist-to-turnover ratio seasons in league history by the time I'd retired. That meant I'd racked up lots of assists, and I knew how to protect and dish the rock. I played in 889 total games, notching a career average of 7.7 points, 2.6 rebounds, and 7.6 assists. My career highs in those categories were 24 points, 19 assists, 10 rebounds, and seven steals in various seasons. My teams made the playoffs five times, and I averaged 8.9 points, 5.6 assists, 2.7 rebounds, and 1.7

steals in those 19 contests. I'd also been to the playoffs five times with three different teams.

For my NBA career, I made about $18.5 million in salary and a few more in endorsements. But what I remember most from my 14 years was going up against the best in the world every day in practice and in the 82-game seasons. Whether it was my friend Spud Webb, idols Magic Johnson and Isiah Thomas, newcomers like Allen Iverson, or old stalwarts like Michael Jordan or Ewing, to play and excel in the NBA was a dream come true. I'd worked my entire life for it, ever since getting that first rubber basketball at three years old. I had some great teammates along the way, too. In a way, there were too many to count, but I do have to mention Alonzo Mourning, Larry Johnson, Rex Chapman, Manute Bol, Moses Malone, David Wingate, Earl Cureton, Charles Oakley, Vince Carter, Tracy McGrady, and Jackson. And, of course, Dell Curry. I'd truly been blessed. Part of me wished I could go back and run one more year in the league, but I knew my time was up.

As they say, Father Time is and always will be undefeated. Yet, the following NBA season, I got a kick out of seeing Jordan come back and play in the league with the Washington Wizards. Jordan was now an old man out there, but he could still teach the young guys something. In the '90s Jordan's father had been murdered, but somehow he'd summoned the courage to keep playing in the league. I admired him for that. I knew I couldn't play in the NBA anymore. Maybe I could coach or work for a team. But at that point, I couldn't even have been a successful little league baseball coach. I still felt deep grief after losing my mother. I tried to stay busy around the house, but it all weighed me down. Thank goodness Chuckie was there for me. While I called my kids every day, sometimes twice a day, everything hurt.

Yet somehow I took a job around then that surprised even me. Though it was hard to get out of bed in the morning, my agent convinced me to take a small part in a new movie. He thought it would be good for me and my career. I still can't believe I took the role, but I'm glad I did. The movie was *Juwanna Mann*. It starred Miguel Núñez Jr. as Jamal Jefferies, a professional basketball player who was kicked off his team. So he decided to disguise himself and play for a woman's professional team. While doing so he fell in love with one of his teammates, and comedy ensued. Although the plot was ridiculous, I liked working with the cast. There were some great people in the movie, including the marvelous Vivica A. Fox, successful rappers Ginuwine and Lil' Kim, comedian Tommy Davidson, and a few NBA players like my old teammate Vlade Divac, Rasheed Wallace, and Dikembe Mutombo. It was a gas.

In the movie I played a guy named Andrew Stewart, one of the other professional players who knew Jamal. Although the critics didn't love the 2002 movie, I still laugh thinking about my time on set. It took my mind of things at home for a while. My agent had been right about that. In fact, that's one of the reasons I do commercials and things like that. It's fun. As time passed, television and film became more and more a part of my family's life. Some people play the game Six Degrees of Kevin Bacon game. Well, I believe you could do the same with me! Sometimes, I felt like the Forrest Gump of NBA players in that I've been connected to so many important parts of the game's history, from Malone to Jordan, Kobe Bryant, Carter, Chris Paul, and Seth and Steph Curry. It's been a blessing from that respect.

As Kim continued to establish herself in her career, she began to earn more opportunities in television. Although we hadn't yet completely reconciled, I was still glad for her. She was doing really well in everything she'd ever wanted. For so long people knew her only as "Muggsy's wife." Then Kim made her own name and she was really good at it. At first, it began with the critically acclaimed television show, *The Wire*, which was based and filmed in Baltimore, where Kim and I had first met. After we'd divorced Kim had moved from New York City to Baltimore to be closer to her father as he struggled with his battle with cancer. After he'd passed, Kim began her new career in earnest.

After her father died, Kim received a call from an important Baltimore casting director. He'd long worked closely with HBO and showrunner, David Simon. He was casting for Simon's series, *The Wire*. It was short notice, but the casting director asked if Kim would be free soon and remain so for six months. She said that sounded perfect to her. She accepted the job. The show's cast and crew became Kim's second family. She grew up professionally working with HBO and Simon. On *The Wire* Kim filled in for one of the main actresses in a hospital bed in Season One and for one of the kids who stole a car in Season Four, among other parts. In 2007 by the show's fifth season, Kim had risen to become a chef for HBO. The actresses Drew Barrymore and Scarlett Johansson had showed her how to make a lot of money cooking, so Kim got her culinary degree and eventually became the personal chef for the great comedic actor, Julia Louis-Dreyfus, on the show *Veep*. Kim used to go shopping with her mother to get the ingredients. It was amazing to see her climb the ladder.

Though hers was more of an impressive regular role, we would both have connections to HBO shows. Some years after *Juwanna Mann*, I took another acting role. This time it was for *Curb Your Enthusiasm*. The show starred Larry David, who was one of the co-creators of the hit NBC show *Seinfeld*. My role was just a small cameo, but it was a fun day. David's character was in the bathroom talking with his friend played by comedian Richard Lewis. It was a crass scene; the two talked about women who were used to dating Black men and the...*ahem*...potential size difference between those men and David. All of a sudden, I walk into the bathroom and use the urinal. Of course, David tries to look and see what I was working with. I see him looking at me and I pretend to get really angry, like I'm about to punch him. Then he practically has a heart attack, so I go easy on him. The whole thing was pretty funny. Off camera, those guys had me crying with laughter. Much of the show is improvised so much of the day was just joking around. In the scene Lewis called me "one of the great guards of all time." He and David are big Knicks fans, but I forgave them for that.

While I tried to figure out my next steps forward in life, I always made sure to keep in contact with my kids. My No. 1 priority was to remain present in their lives any way that I could, no matter physical distance. Tyisha was doing well in Baltimore. She was starting her career in social work and would soon own her own business. Brittney was starting college, and Ty was starting high school. Kim and I still weren't talking much, but I always just wanted her to be happy. During her time acting, she started dating again. She'd gotten close with a man who worked on one of her sets at HBO as a director of production. I hoped they would be happy together. At the time I was also dating.

I'd started seeing someone around the time I shot the *Curb* episode. Her name was Sharon Smith, and we'd gotten pretty serious. We'd met in 2003. Sharon was a beautiful person and an excellent mother to her three children. We dated for several years and got into a real groove together. We even settled down and were going to make a life together. We'd talked about engagement, marriage. But only a few years into our relationship, Sharon was diagnosed with breast cancer. In 2009 she died from it, and it broke my heart. Once that happened I was in a completely dark place. I was so morose. It screwed my head up just as I was beginning to find solid footing. Ty came to Charlotte around then. He was a high school student, and Kim and I agreed that he should be with his father at this time in his life. But that was a difficult time for both of us. Ty went through some tough moments here in Charlotte. As I drifted, so did he. He was a basketball player growing up, a solid guard on his AAU team. But Ty wasn't helping his future by the way he acted. Ty began to rebel.

He told me he didn't want to live with me anymore. Like a lot of teen-agers, he had a small run-in with the law over alcohol. He was pulled over with an open container in his car. When Kim got the call that Ty was in trouble, she came down to Charlotte. She and I talked to the prosecutor, who recognized Ty's last name from the file. The prosecutor said he would offer Ty, who wasn't yet 18 years old, a scared straight tactic. He'd have Ty walk out of the courtroom in handcuffs and, thankfully, right into our custody. That tactic absolutely worked. It changed his whole life around.

After that ordeal Kim agreed to stay in Charlotte to help me raise Ty. She gave up her New York City Upper East Side apartment she loved (though the kids didn't) and a romantic relationship to come back. We'd been pretty mad at one another, but that quickly began to fade as she spent more time in Charlotte. Almost immediately after that, Ty's grades improved. He'd later go on to a job working with the Hornets' marketing department.

At some point along the way, Kim realized I still needed her, too. We needed each other. When she came back down to Charlotte to help with Ty, I was also at my wit's end. She'd been gone for 10 years, and I was barely holding onto my sanity. So Kim agreed to stay—first to help Ty and then to help me. Our decade apart had helped heal old wounds. Soon, Kim and I started to realize we were still in love. We became romantically involved. We went on dates together again. We talked about how we'd gotten married at such a young age before we really knew who we were as people. She told me how she'd needed space to grow and create her own identity in the world. As we got older, we had more perspective, which allowed us to start fresh as a family. There was reason to hope.

MEMORY LANE
Kim Bogues

"David Simon is the coolest man ever. Before he did *The Wire*, he was a writer for *The Baltimore Sun* newspaper. He lived in Baltimore the whole time he was making the show. I had the biggest respect for him because he lived what he wrote about. We broke records filming that show. We worked six days a week, 12-to-14 hours a day. It still makes me laugh that we were never nominated for an Emmy. *The Wire* is hands down the best television show ever. We really became a close family because we were all nobodies at that time. I was Kima's [played by Sonja Sohn] body double. I remember she was going to walk at the end of the first season because she wanted more pay. So they wrote that into the script; they shot her. They were going to kill her off. So, when she's laying there in the hospital bed, that's actually me! Sonja was out negotiating her contract. Working on set, making great pay, that really helped me to grow into the woman I am today. It helped to give me my own identity."

17

COACH MUGGSY

THE STORY OF CHARLOTTE PROFESSIONAL BASKETBALL GETS PRETTY difficult to track after I retired from the league in 2001. With the conclusion of the 2001–02 season, the NBA decided to approve a permanent move for the team to relocate 715 miles west from Charlotte to New Orleans. That irked me. It was nothing against New Orleans, which is a beautiful city. But the Hornets have always belonged in Charlotte. We'd broken attendance records with the team in the mid-1990s, and no one could tell me that they couldn't be a great draw again. There were, though, reasons outside of basketball for the move. In 2002 attendance was down, but that was largely because the people of Charlotte were upset and fed up with the organization and its owner, George Shinn. Not only had the team traded away Alonzo Mourning, Larry Johnson, and me, but there were serious rumblings that Shinn was involved in a messy personal dispute.

He was accused of some misconduct, and though he was ultimately found innocent, a very public trial hurt his legacy, especially in Charlotte. Shinn decided to leave the public eye and he moved the Hornets to New Orleans. He eventually sold his ownership share in 2010 for $300 million, which was 10 times what he'd originally paid. With the Hornets in New Orleans, the NBA looked to bring another professional team back to the basketball-hungry city of Charlotte. In 2003 Robert Johnson, founder of popular television channel BET, bought the rights to Charlotte's new professional team. He decided to name the team the Charlotte Bobcats, which many thought was a nod to his own first name. Nevertheless, in that moment, Johnson became the first majority Black owner in U.S major pro sports. I was happy for that. Johnson paid $300 million to join the league, the same Shinn received to leave it.

In the 2004 expansion draft, just 16 years after Dell Curry and I had been selected in the Hornets expansion draft, the Bobcats began to fill out their team. That summer in the amateur draft, the team selected the talented big man, Emeka Okafor, from the University of Connecticut. He would go on to win Rookie of the Year despite the team finishing 18–64 in its inaugural season. In 2005 while still the New Orleans Hornets, that team selected my old friend and all-world guard, Chris Paul. He has always been an amazing player. I am happy to say I taught Paul a few aspects of the game. I love that guy. But after drafting Paul, the Hornets' good fortune would quickly turn. Just a few short months after the draft, the devastating Hurricane Katrina struck New Orleans. The team had to relocate 575 miles west for two years to Oklahoma City as New Orleans recovered.

The team played two seasons as the New Orleans/Oklahoma City Hornets, and the city got such a taste for professional basketball that a year after the Hornets moved back to New Orleans, Oklahoma City acquired the Seattle SuperSonics from the Northwest. Later after moving back to New Orleans, the Hornets traded Paul to the Los Angeles Clippers (after trying to trade him to the Los Angeles Lakers). In 2012 the Hornets drafted star big man Anthony Davis, but seven years later after little success, they traded him to the Lakers to play with LeBron James and win championships. But it doesn't end there! In 2010 Johnson sold the Bobcats to Michael Jordan. My old NBA colleague was taking over my old team. Previously, Jordan had a minority ownership stake in the Washington Wizards that he got when he came back to play for Washington after his 1998 retirement from the Chicago Bulls. But Jordan sold that stake so that he could become the majority owner of the Charlotte Bobcats.

During the 2009–10 season, the Charlotte Bobcats made the playoffs for the first time and boasted their first All-Star, Gerald Wallace. But while the city was happy for the team, the name never felt like it fit. In 2012 the New Orleans Hornets decided to change the franchise's name. At first New Orleans asked if the Utah Jazz would give back the Jazz moniker back after the New Orleans Jazz had relocated to Utah in 1979. But Utah declined. So, New Orleans sought a new locally-inspired name. In 2012 the team landed on the Pelicans, which is Louisiana's state bird. In 2013–14 the New Orleans Pelicans played their first official season, which allowed the Charlotte Bobcats to finally change their name back to the Charlotte Hornets.

But the Bobcats and Hornets aren't the only two professional teams in Charlotte's modern-day hoops history. When discussing the city's professional basketball, the WNBA's Charlotte Sting must also be considered. The WNBA, which launched in 1997, has become one of the most important sports leagues in America. Some give the league a hard time, but they forget the league is still young, only 25 years old. When the NBA was 25 years old, it wasn't on particularly sturdy ground. But the WNBA has grown thanks to stars like Sue Bird, Candace Parker, and Ivory Latta. And I'm proud to say that in 2005, I joined the WNBA as the new head coach of the Charlotte Sting. It turned out to be an opportunity I'll cherish forever. One of the original WNBA teams, the Sting was the sister squad of the Hornets. Johnson took over ownership of the Sting in 2003. Just four years prior, the team drafted the franchise's all-time best player, a legend, and five-time WNBA All-Star in Dawn Staley. She played for the Sting until 2005 and was a standout in all senses of the word.

I was named the team's head coach midway through 2005. Although I never got a chance to coach Staley—the team traded her to the Houston Comets 23 games into the season and just two days before I took over—the legacy of the three-time Olympic gold medalist lives on in Charlotte. I stewarded the team for a year-plus. Our 5'6" point guard Helen Darling was the closest player to my height. Sadly, we were pretty bad in 2005 record-wise. We finished 6–28, though I only got there for the last 10 games or so. Nevertheless, I tried to keep things light in practices. It was a good group of women who were very talented and professional through and through. Their fundamentals were off the charts and better than many NBA players. As mothers, sisters, wives, and daughters, they all had so much respect for the game. We worked hard, but we goofed around some, too.

We finished every practice with a half-court shot competition. I wanted to set a good foundation for the team, one where they were happy to come to work. It helped some because we were better the following year but still we weren't great. The following season, we brought the record up to 11–23, but it wasn't enough to keep interest in the team throughout the city. The WNBA was new and hadn't found the traction it needed yet. After that year Johnson announced the Sting would be no more. Like the Hornets, the Sting never made it to the Finals, but they did post some exciting seasons and some good playoff runs. When I coached, we had one All-Star, forward Tangela Smith, and I'd developed good relationships with other players like Darling and Allison Feaster. But we just didn't have enough time to build before the team folded in 2007.

The opportunity had given me some stability. I loved my players and I realized I'd needed the routine of the basketball season. Working with the Sting was an important moment in my life, and I'll always remain grateful for it. The women I coached were terrific. That gave me hope for the growth of the WNBA game. The players are even more athletic than when I coached. They're dunking with regularity while also impacting important social conversations. It's admirable, especially given the long odds the league faced at its outset from folks who disparaged the women's game without even thinking. It takes time to build anything good that will last. Each year the WNBA gets stronger, which in turns helps to inspire and produce stronger younger players. David Stern knew what he was doing when he helped launch the league. Kudos to him for that.

After I'd left the NBA, I was working hard to build my own professional second act. In that way, I was in search of solid ground. I tried my hand at real estate. I invested in properties around Charlotte and the state of North Carolina. I liked that enough, but it never really thrilled me. I still own a few of those properties, but I've sold a lot of them. After my coaching career with the Sting folded, I did some radio play-by-play for games and some more speaking engagements. I also conducted basketball camps, which I liked. My goal was to keep busy and stay as productive as possible. With Kim now back in my life, I felt a renewed drive to be productive. Life had been hard for a while, but I'd done enough wallowing. I owed it to Kim and our kids to thrive and be the best person I could.

In 2011 I took another coaching opportunity. The United Faith Christian Academy Charlotte hired me to coach the high school's boys basketball team. I'd served as an assistant for the team for a few years under the former coach, Shaun Wiseman, but then I'd accepted the head job. I'd had so many great teachers throughout my life—from my mother to Coach Howard and Coach Wade—that I knew the importance of good direction for young people. I knew what it could mean to a student-athlete to be shown the game and taught it at a high level. I coached the United Faith Christian Academy Falcons for three seasons, mentoring my players to be the best of my abilities. Education is very important. In my mind the only poor people are those without education. I knew what it was like to dedicate your life to the game of basketball at an early age and work every hour toward learning and getting better. I wanted to help the kids.

We had some great players over those three years at United Faith. We graduated six all-state players. Some guys went on to to play Division I and pro basketball later in their careers, including the 6'1" guard, Braxton Ogbueze, and the big seven-footer, Peter Jurkin, who came to Charlotte from South Sudan. Jurkin eventually became a part of my family, too, though we didn't officially adopt him. He had enrolled in United Faith through a youth student-athlete program. When he got to school in 2009, I was still an assistant with the team. Seeing how much shorter I was, he was immediately skeptical that I could teach him anything about basketball. But I quickly showed him how much I could help him adjust to life both on and off the court. When he arrived Jurkin didn't speak much English. But he was a fast learner. As a player Jurkin did very well in high school and he went on to play internationally for a few countries overseas.

Jurkin now runs his own restaurant business in Texas, which has multiple locations. Sometimes it's small acts of kindness that can make all the difference in someone's life. He is just one of the reasons why my time at United Faith was a blessing. When I think about my relationship to the game of basketball, I think of myself as a teacher as much as I do a player.

I've run and been a guest at numerous basketball camps and I've traveled to places like the Philippines, Turkey, Guam, and China, all of which absolutely adore the NBA. I've taught the game in all those places. When you're my size, you have to learn a lot to succeed. So, I tell all my players: take small steps and don't skip any. Before you know it, you'll get there. Visualize it and put the work in. I had a great deal of natural talent, of course, but I had to learn how to apply it in every way I could find.

United Faith offered me a chance to continue coaching, but I decided to follow some other opportunities in life. Nevertheless, I'll always remember that a great many coaches have helped me and I'll never forget them for what they did for me in my life along the way. People like Bob Wade at Dunbar High, Coach Howard at the rec center, and Coach Nestor at Wake Forest were instrumental. One of the (few) things that's good about getting older is that you're able to look at the generation of people younger than you and learn from them, too. As a coach I've learned a lot from my players over the years—from the kids at my camps to the players on the Sting to the young men at United Faith Christian Academy. Like my best coaches have said to me, I told each and every one of my players that I'd be there for them after the final buzzer or after they play their last game. In the end these connections are what are most important.

MEMORY LANE
Helen Darling

"I remember we had one of those posters of Muggsy when he joined the team. We were playing bad at the time. And we colored in his teeth and gave him glasses and devil horns. We thought it was so funny, but he was so pissed about it at the time! He cussed us out and used some choice words. He was like, 'Y'all play too much!' I was dying laughing. We still joke about it to this day. I also remember that at the end of the year, I was like, 'Muggsy! We need to throw an end-of-the year party!' So he rented limos for us all and made us feel really special. He did it also to build trust, to let us know that: hey, we work hard and we play hard. There was a respect factor there. It was so funny. We ended up winning like 10 games that year, but we had an end-of-the-year celebration like we'd won the WNBA championship! He was definitely like my godfather. He'd tell me what I was doing wrong if he saw me get out of line. He'd say, 'Come on now, point guard!' It was subtle things—not in the way like a father—but still concerned. It was definitely a blessing to have him there. When I think of him now, I think of a man with courage, determination despite the odds, and just a very contagious personality to uplift others."

18

WHAT'S OLD
IS NEW

I HAD NO IDEA WHAT KIM AND BRITTNEY WERE PLANNING FOR ME. TO BE honest, I didn't know they were planning anything at all. They were pretty hush-hush about the whole thing. But I should have known. Kim's always had a flare for the grand and the dramatic, and I love her for it. At the time Brittney was working as an event planner, so she was at the top of her game when it came to making a party sing. I should have guessed that they had something up their sleeves. But honestly, I really had no clue. In the end Kim and Brittney surprised me with one of the best days of my life on my 50th birthday on January 9, 2015. Originally, they'd said they had a little dinner planned for me with a few friends, including Dell and Sonya Curry. Kim and I were now fully back together. We were in love and appreciative to be in each other's lives again. We'd talked about marriage but hadn't set a date.

I had, however, gone to the Charlotte courthouse to pick up a marriage certificate. We were both very busy at the time. I'd left my job coaching United Faith Christian Academy in 2014 to take a job as an official Charlotte Hornets ambassador. Now that the team was back in Charlotte and named the Hornets again, the franchise and I had made amends. I'd been angry with the team for years after they'd traded me. In life, though, we have to learn to let go of certain things that don't serve us. Now as far as the team and I were concerned, that was all water under the bridge. How could I stay mad? Michael Jordan had brought the Hornets back, and all was right in the world of Charlotte basketball again. Personally, I was thankful Jordan had done that. It's funny that he's the owner now. Talk about worlds colliding. I'd played against him for more than a decade, and then he became my boss with the team.

For the past few years, there's been a rumor about Jordan and me that I need to address. I think it sparked when we played the Chicago Bulls in Charlotte after Jordan had come back from his first retirement. Someone for some reason said that Jordan had yelled to me, "Shoot the ball, midget!" in a game, and that for some reason, my career had never been the same as a result. The thought was that Jordan got in my head by calling me a midget, and that I lost my talent. If true, it was like the Monstars had zapped me all over again! But for the record, let me just say that the idea is preposterous. It's actually asinine. First of all, Jordan never said that to me. Second, I'd like to tell all the folks, who believe that happened, to just take a moment to reflect. From all that I've gone through in my life, should anyone believe that any person saying any word would get me off my game? That's like hunting a duck with a water gun. Third, I played seven seasons after Jordan allegedly said that.

I grew up and played in Baltimore as a 5'3" point guard of a back-to-back undefeated, championship-winning team. I've heard every dictionary and thesaurus word when it comes to trash talking. Not to mention, Jordan and I have a strong respect for one another. We're NBA veterans. We clashed in the playoffs and we did a lot for the state of professional basketball in North Carolina. No matter our height, we saw eye to eye as men. So, offended by a word? No way! Not a chance.

What I did have to get over, however, was my initial anger with the Hornets franchise. The team never should have moved to New Orleans. When George Shinn moved the organization, I was heartbroken. It took a decade for Shinn and I to make up. But I'm glad we did. Holding onto anger is never good. As difficult as it can be, reconciliation is an important part of life. Shinn and I took part in a photo shoot together in 2013 for the Hornets' 25th anniversary celebration. It was the first time we were in a room together since 1997. We hugged and said we were glad to see one another. We posed for pictures back to back. Things had come full circle, and I was glad to be on good terms with the franchise again. When they offered me the official team ambassador position, I was proud to take it. I was there from Day One of the expansion and now I was back with the team's second installment. The mayor of Charlotte gave me a key to the city, too. All of that was tremendous. But nothing could compare to Kim giving me her hand in marriage. Kim was deep into her career, too. We'd talked about getting remarried, but we didn't know when there was the proper time. She was the personal chef for *Veep* on HBO, and I wanted her to have all the time she needed to keep her career flourishing.

But that's when the surprise happened right under my nose. Just as I'd come full circle with the Hornets, Kim and I were set to do that as well. She and Brittney had seen to that. What I thought was a small gathering of friends turned out to be our wedding day all over again. On January 9, 2015, I remarried the love of my life. Kim had invited 70 of our closest friends, and they'd all been waiting for me in a top floor apartment in a fancy Charlotte high-rise building. The great Moses Malone was there and so were Reggie Williams, Shinn, Brittney, Ty Jr., Sherron, Chuckie, Dell, and Sonya, Kim's family, teammates, coaches, and everyone that I loved. Most of all, Kim was there. Thankfully, I was dressed for the night. I thought we were going to a nice dinner uptown. But when I opened the door of our friend's apartment, I saw everyone's smiling faces looking at Kim and me as we walked in.

Cell phone cameras instantly popped off. Gosh, Kim looked so beautiful. At the altar I stared into her big brown eyes and thought about how lucky I was to be with her again. Surrounded by friends and family, we stood at the altar. Kim and Brittney had been planning it for more than seven months. Amidst tears and blowing noses, we said our vows. I told Kim I would be a better husband and better person than I ever was before. We'd started together when we had nothing. Then we lost each other. Few get this kind of second chance, and we were fortunate enough to try again. I thanked God for allowing us back in each other's lives. Kim had loved me as a snotty-nosed kid in 1987, and here I was again, just a snotty-nosed kid, crying for her. I leaned in to kiss her, but Kim stopped me. Of course, she had her own vows first. She told me she'd always loved me and that she always would love me. She told me she wanted to spend the rest of her life with me, and now that we'd both grown up, we would be better for each other and for our family than ever before.

My heart felt full holding her hands on the altar. Suddenly I realized I didn't have a ring. But Ty turned to me and held one out. We both said "I do" and we kissed. Then we celebrated! It was great to see my friends. That was the last day I ever saw Malone. Sadly, the Big Fella passed away eight months later at 60 years old. Perhaps more than any player, Malone had made an impact on me. Not a day goes by when I don't think about the Big Fella. But even before his passing, I experienced another of the hardest losses of my entire life. It was like losing my mother all over again. In the summer of 2015, just a few months after my second wedding with Kim, my sister, Sherron, lost her battle with cancer and passed away at 55 years old. To say that was tough would be an understatement. My mother and my sister were more influential on me than anyone in the world. Without them, there would be no Muggsy Bogues.

My mother and my sister gave me the strength to be who I was. For them both to be gone, that hurt like a thousand daggers. But before she left this world, Sherron fought. My sister was the only person I'd ever heard of who walked out of hospice care. We took Sherron to hospice in June of 2015 before her birthday that month. But Sherron wasn't having it! I laugh thinking about it. My dear sister was so determined to spend her June 27th birthday at home that she summoned the strength and up and walked out of hospice care. She said she was feeling better and so she got herself to our home and stayed with us for her birthday. We got to celebrate with her one last time. Since Sherron was so set on being home, the doctors said there was nothing they could do to stop her. She walked out on June 26, and we threw a birthday party for her with a cake and everything. She stayed with us for a few more days, and then we had to take her back. Sherron passed away shortly after.

She was a fighter, another pistol just like my mother. I can still hear her voice in that loud gym, "Muggsy!" she would yell. "Shoot it! Shoot the ball! Listen to your coach and shoot!" She wanted nothing more than for me to succeed. God bless her. She was my best friend. Life was hard again for a while after that. It helped tremendously to have Kim with me. Now that we were married, our relationship felt stronger than ever. I knew I had to stay strong with her. My relationship with the Hornets helped. About six long months after Sherron passed, I was invited to participate in the 2016 NBA All-Star weekend in Toronto. The league recruited me to play in the celebrity game with other legends like Chauncey Billups, Tracy McGrady, Rick Fox, and Elena Delle Donne, and big-name celebrities like Anthony Anderson, O'Shea Jackson Jr., and Jason Sudeikis. It was fun to get on the court again and make a few moves. But my muscles felt it the next day. My team's coach was the funny comedian, Kevin Hart, who shed his suit halfway through and substituted himself in the game wearing my number!

I shouldn't have let him get away with that. Needless to say, we lost to the other squad coached by the great singer, Drake. But Hart and I had a good time together; he was about the only one out there my height! Later he called me an "NBA legend," which I thought was cool, of course. That same year I appeared in an episode of the USA medical television show, *Royal Pains*. In fact, I was around cameras a lot around then. ESPN decided to make a documentary about my Dunbar High team for the channel's 30 for 30 series. They wanted to know all about Reggie Lewis, David Wingate, and, of course, Russ in high school, and what it was like to never lose and grow up in Baltimore. Coincidentally, in 2016, I was also nominated for the first time for the Basketball Hall of Fame. Although I have yet to get in, my hope is that one day the Hall of Fame will recognize me, and I'll be remembered with the other greats of the game. When I think about my career, how I retired 12th all time in assists, how the Hornets were as big as Nirvana, I feel I deserve to be in there. But that's not my decision to make.

Later in 2017 ESPN released *Baltimore Boys*. Watching the documentary brought tears to my eyes. My friends and I went through so much together—so many ups and downs—that to see them all there at once really moved me. I try to look forward. But on those rare occasions when I look back and remember the story, I realize how much had to happen for me to become who I became. It's been a blessing, and I hope it's inspired people along the way. Our team's story is so unique and important for the history of the game, especially in Baltimore. In 2019 I did a bunch of ads for the web hosting company, GoDaddy. That same year the NBA held the annual All-Star Game in Charlotte for the first time since February 10, 1991. I was invited back to the fan festivities, and it made my heart full to see my city celebrated on a national stage. The Hornets played our first season in 1988–89, so to have the league's All-Star Game there 30 years later was a gift. It was like seeing a close friend blow out the candles at his 30th birthday party.

It was great to see the Hornets' best player, Kemba Walker, play in the All-Star Game that year. He was a starter, too. Walker was a shorter player (not as short as me, of course), but he could really hoop. He had a great step-back jump shot from the foul-line elbow. He played quick, was a pest on defense, and had a knack for the big games. Sound familiar? All in all, the festivities felt rather blissful. There are a lot of moments I can point to in my life that have put a smile on my face, but the 2019 NBA All-Star Game stands out clearly as one of them in recent memory. There was a time when I wondered if I'd ever reconcile with the team. Heck, there was a time when I wasn't sure if the Hornets would ever reside in Charlotte again. But the man upstairs works in mysterious ways, and I'm thankful for reconciliations and renewed relationships.

MEMORY LANE
Chris Paul

"Muggsy used to host a basketball camp up the street from my house at Charlotte Country Day. When I was young before I went to college, Muggsy would have me come over and speak to his camp. I used to spend some time with him. Muggsy used to tell me how he used to steal the ball all the time. It's crazy; I don't think he's talked about enough. In Charlotte everybody knows him, but around the league, I think he's somebody that should be appreciated a lot more. Muggs has always been one of the most selfless guys you'll ever meet, the coolest, most laid-back. He was probably the first NBA player that I ever knew. I appreciate him wholeheartedly for that, for his mentorship of me at an early age."

19

PERSPECTIVE

THE FIRST MEMORY I CAN RECALL IS STANDING ON TOP OF A LARGE staircase in the Lafayette Court Housing Projects. It was the location of my first big adventure. I was two years old, small as ever. I threw my bottle down the long staircase. It must have fell 10 stories. So I began to climb down to get it step by step, slowly but surely. By the time I got all the way to the bottom to get my bottle, I didn't realize how far I'd traveled. But I now had to get back up. I was just two years old, but I remember that my mom slapped my butt for that. Most of all, I remember that feeling in the pit of my stomach, telling me that I had to get moving. I had that drive early on. Now people call me "Chairman Bogues" because I have my nonprofit foundation.

Brittney and I run the Muggsy Bogues Family Foundation, which focuses on job training for young people. When people think of scholarships, we often think of sending people to Harvard or Yale, and that's well and fine. But some kids learn better and will do better for their communities by learning how to be plumbers, mechanics, or any number of other respectable trades. So we want to help them succeed. To do so, we started the foundation with my mom in 1999, but I let it go by the wayside after she'd passed. Thankfully, Brittney has breathed new life into it, and it's going stronger than ever. My hope is that if we can strengthen families, we can make the world a better place for everyone. Giving folks hope is so important. That's my calling. So many people are afraid to do what they want in their heart. Giving them a helping hand can make the difference. I know it helped me.

We get letters from people around the world who are in tough situations. Sometimes they're on their deathbeds and they just need a little hope. Some of them ask me to send a video or just say hello. But what's really touched my heart is when Brittney told me that after seeing what I've done, she believes in her heart that anything is possible. Knowing that I've helped my daughter in this way pushes me to keep going. It makes me feel like I can't give up now. Like me, Brittney is also a proud Wake Forest album (class of '09) and she knows what hard work is about. My son, Ty Jr., is excelling, too. He works full time with the Charlotte Hornets in the marketing department, player outreach, and youth development. Tyisha is doing great, too. She owns her own business and is a social worker in Baltimore. That's no small endeavor. I'm so proud of all that my children have accomplished. They didn't have the easiest road growing up, but they've made themselves into mighty fine adults.

Even though I got a lot of help, I also worked hard throughout my life. Today I'm at the stage now when I can sit back and reflect on much of it. When you're forging your way, it can be difficult to keep a bird's-eye view on the whole thing, so to speak. But thankfully, I have perspective now and I can admit that I feel true amazement when I think about all I've done in this world. I've been on some great teams, had some great teammates. I got to match up against the best in the world for 14 years in the league and for several more in college before that. I earned the respect of my peers, which is the cherry on top. Being the height I am, still being the smallest player ever to make the NBA, makes me feel proud. It gives me hope that I've inspired people who've seen me play. I like to believe I've helped a lot of kids along the way, and that just makes my heart feel full.

To pass the time these days, I like to play chess; hang out with my dog, Dunbar; watch Netflix; and play Nintendo Wii Boxing. Chuckie thinks he can hang with me, but he absolutely cannot. I also play a lot of Scrabble. I can get pretty competitive in those, but it's all in good fun. I also regularly record a new podcast with my friends, Charles Oakley and Earl Cureton, called *3 Leagues OGs*. We have guests on like our old friends Vince Carter, Tracy McGrady, Rex Chapman, Alonzo Mourning, and Dr. J. It's a great way to keep in touch with my friends. We tell stories about the good ol' days. In my spare time, I still watch a lot of new basketball, too. I try to watch the Hornets whenever I can. Right now, we have a young point guard, LaMelo Ball, who is looking strong in his first couple of years. Plus, the team brought back the teal pinstripe uniforms, which you know I love. I like to watch Seth and Steph Curry as they tear through the league, too. I also recently enjoyed watching Darnell Rogers, a 5'2" guard at the University of Maryland Baltimore County. He's now the shortest scholarship player to ever play in the NCAA. I have my fingers crossed for him.

In 2020 I was inducted into the North Carolina Sports Hall of Fame. I'm going to be 60 years old soon and, though I could still teach these guys a thing or two about the game, I know the NBA is in good hands. When I came into the league, my favorite guard was Magic Johnson. He was 6'9", but I didn't care about his height when I watched him. Instead, I studied how he set his guys up, how he always kept a positive attitude on the court, how he had a knack for the flashy side of the game but also for the purity of it. The way Magic ran the floor has never been duplicated. I also loved the great Isiah Thomas. He was shorter, only about 6'0" tall. I watched him maneuver and score amongst the trees under the basket and the way he willed his team to victory after victory. In many ways I modeled myself after both these men. But I also modeled myself after people like Dwayne Wood. I learned a lot from Tim Hardaway, John Stockton, Kevin Johnson, and Mark Jackson. Though, I'm no longer playing, I continue to learn from players like Steph Curry and LaMelo Ball.

Truly, I hope they can learn something from me, too. Curry and the Golden State Warriors ushered in smallball, and it was a whirlwind to watch. At the time, while the Warriors were winning championships, I couldn't help but see my own basketball DNA in those games. *Push the ball, make the extra pass.* But smallball isn't just for guards. It gives any undersized player the chance to play bigger and prove they belong. I love that smallball has taken over the league. I'm glad coaches are utilizing it more and more as a strategy to win and showcase their most skilled players. The Warriors made it a household name, but it had begun long before Warriors coach Steve Kerr called a play. It started with guys like Spud Webb. It continued with Greg Grant, Earl Boykins, and me. It's grown into a phenomenon, and the success of smallball indicates that the game is both relevant and available for anyone who wants to play it. All you need is a ball.

People are always amazed that I was able to play in the league at my height, but basketball was always available to me. That's the beauty of the game, and it always will be. As I watch the NBA today, sometimes I wonder what it would be like to play in a game during the current smallball era. I think I'd do pretty well, to be honest. I think any NBA player can play in any era. But there were a lot of different rules when I played, which stifled pace and point scoring. Now those are gone in large part. There's more space to maneuver, and seven footers are bringing the ball up the court. I think I'd be able to get to the rim better to penetrate and dish. I think I'd rack up many more assists! Perhaps if I played today instead of in the '90s, people might think differently about me. With all of the opportunities point guards get to handle, pass, and shoot, my numbers could look even better. It's fun to daydream. We all have a journey, a path to follow. And I loved just about every minute of my career. But it all just makes me wonder.

More important than my basketball career, though, I'm proud of my family. Another one of the (few) benefits of getting older is your grandchildren. Thankfully, Tyisha has a son who loves basketball, and it just tickles me. My grandson, Samartine (who people called "Fat Man") was 11 years old in 2015 when he became Internet famous. He could handle the ball like his Grandpa Muggsy. In fact, a few of his videos went viral. As he's gotten older, I've been able to teach my grandson the game, how to protect the basketball, how to use it as a tool to get around a defender and into the lane. I taught him how to play bigger than his size. He's part of the Bogues family tree, so you know he's no giant. But he can still play and affect the game in positive ways. I tell him that it doesn't matter how tall he is. Just look at me or look at Webb.

Samartine got his first scholarship offer in 2020 as a freshman in high school. Now a junior, he's the starting point guard at Calvert Hall High. That makes me so happy; I can't even put it into words. People say I'm one of a kind. For me, it's about inspiring others. Now, as smallball takes over the game, perhaps my grandson will get a fair look and a chance to succeed on the next level even if he is shorter. I always tell him there's no such thing as a light switch when it comes to hard work. It's a constant effort. First and foremost, I believe life is about personal growth. But it's also about how we each impact the world around us through that growth. As my game improved, I was able to provide an example to so many, like my grandson and Steph and Seth Curry. Although Chris Paul's or Steph Curry's games may have blossomed to the All-Star status without my influence, I know that I made a big impact on my grandson. That legacy will continue to impact the game. I've seen it before and I will see it happen again.

Thankfully, growing up, my grandson didn't have to endure the same ridicule I did. He didn't have to hear the same awful jokes about his size. He didn't have to fight the opinions of the whole neighborhood to get in the game like I did at his age. My grandson didn't have to witness the horrible things I did, either. Instead, he just got to be a kid, which is what he and any young person deserves.

MEMORY LANE
Tyisha Bogues

"My dad was a person who came from a horrible neighborhood. It was drug-infested; there was poverty everywhere. And he still made it. He pushed through, undersized. Everywhere he looked, he heard, 'You can't do this, you can't do that!' Yet, he won championships in high school. He got a Division I scholarship, a full ride. He was drafted and had a 14-year NBA career. Today, my son is 16 years old and he's an inch taller than my dad. But no one doubts his ability as a basketball player. That's the impact he had. They just say, 'Oh my god, you play just like your grandfather! Just like Muggsy!' When people tell my son that, it lights up his world. That's his hero."

ACKNOWLEDGMENTS

BEFORE ANYONE ELSE I'D LIKE TO THANK MY MOTHER, LAINEY. WITHOUT her, none of this would be possible. I'd like to thank my sister, Sherron; brothers, Chuckie and Stroh; and my father, Billy, for being family through thick and thin. I want to thank my coaches and teachers, most of all Bob Wade, Leon Howard, and Reggie Williams. I want to thank Wake Forest University, the Washington Bullets, Charlotte Hornets, Golden State Warriors, and Toronto Raptors for believing in me. I want to thank my daughters and my son and my wife, Kim. My life would be much gloomier without you. Finally, for this book, I want to especially thank my daughter, Brittney, and all of the people who helped make it, including the folks at my podcast, *3 League OGs*, and other NBA hubs like the *Lowe Post Podcast* and Charlotte Hornets and Phoenix Suns postgame team, which helped with some of the book's Memory Lanes. *The Boys of Dunbar* and *In the Land of the Giants* also served as helpful references. Thank you for allowing me and my story to grace your proverbial stages. Life is a wild ride, but if you believe in yourself, have faith, and the goodness of your heart, you can achieve great heights.